DOG ALGEBRA

When Positive Reinforcement Fails To Solve The Problem

TAMMIE ROGERS

DEDICATION

I dedicate this book to my husband, Robert, who serves as both my rock and my wings. I love you.

In loving memory of my mother, Carol Johnson.

CONTENTS

ॐॐ

ACKNOWLEDGMENTS

൙൙

I would like to acknowledge all the folks who have come to us for instruction over the years. As you candidly shared your experiences and perceptions about your dogs, I grew a greater understanding of my audience.

My husband, Robert, is my sounding board. He is the keel that keeps things running straight. He is fearless in his interactions with dogs which has permitted us to rehabilitate many dogs that people have written off as impossible. Without his assistance, I could not have learned as much about the most severely anti-social dogs and the people who own them.

I must thank my parents, John and Carol, for raising me right. The older I get, the more I realize how they shaped my views on life.

To Martha Temple, who doggedly worked to help me produce the best quality book I could muster, thank you.

I deeply appreciate the following individuals who reviewed the manuscript:

Cheryl Lethem
Susan Rayfield
Arlene Soderlund

Cover photo by Tammie Rogers

CHAPTER 1

✧

CONTEMPLATION

In Fourth grade I came down with some sort of illness that kept me out of school for a few weeks. So that I would not get too far behind, my mother met with my teacher each day and brought back my homework. For an hour or two every day, I sat at the kitchen table and finished the work. My older sister was charged with the task of delivering the papers back to my teacher in the morning. My mom would speak with the teacher in the afternoon and collect my new assignments.

I was a good kid and a good student. I loved my teachers, and they loved me. If I had been a dog, I would have been a Golden Retriever. I wanted to please. I wanted to do well. I did not want to disappoint my parents or my teachers. I was willing and happy and didn't complain much.

I was accomplished at science and reading and quite proficient at arithmetic, too. However, one afternoon while I was still at home recuperating from my infirmity, I overheard my mother on the phone. She was complaining to a friend about how many math problems my teacher expected me to complete. I heard her say something like, "If she can do ten double-digit-long-division problems, she shouldn't have to do a hundred of them."

It got me thinking. I contemplated how long I sat at that table, by myself, every day, doing all that work. Not to mention, I was sick and all. It was true. Why did I have to do so many math problems? It was as if, in an instant, I rejected arithmetic. It was no longer fun. It was laborious. Yeah, like my mom said! Why did I have to do so much math?

When I was in Costa Rica doing field research during college, I got food poisoning. It was after I ate a shrimp dish at a Chinese restaurant in Limon on the coast. I spent a whole day throwing up and feeling badly when I was supposed to be having fun in the ocean. I didn't make a conscious decision to avoid shrimp in lobster sauce, but it took about ten years before I could eat seafood in oriental cuisine again. I could eat fried shrimp or shrimp scampi. I could eat beef, pork, or chicken Chow Mein, but the psychosomatic process of pairing what happens to the soma (body) with what gets processed in the psyche (brain) is nearly impossible to eject from your subconscious even if you try. It was sort of like that, back in fourth grade, with math. I was injected with the poison (a comment I was never supposed to hear from a highly respected source), and my desire to do math just shut off.

As one can imagine, I didn't do very well in math from that point onwards—that is until I took algebra in high school. For me it was akin to an epiphany. I realize that kids all around the globe learn algebra every year and, for them, it's just another math subject. But I had not permitted myself to learn math since fourth grade, so it truly was a moment of great clarity for me. Algebra made sense. It was so obvious. I didn't understand why anyone would worry about learning algebra. I got it. Balance the equation around an equals sign. How much simpler could it be?

Geometry had rules. You had to learn how many degrees were in a right angle? What's an isosceles triangle? What are the properties of a polygon? How do you determine the volume of an irregular shape? But algebra had one basic premise—the equals sign. Any kid growing up with another sibling understands the equals sign. She got more than me! That's not fair. It doesn't equal!

Algebra is about using logic to solve equations. Things need to balance. While I was fairly artistic as a kid, I also enjoyed the comfort of something being logical. When my little sister and I played "Star Trek" (a game which required the stairway to transport us to a strange new world and new civilization, sometimes referred to as the basement), Cheryl was always Captain Kirk and I was Spock even though I was older. In theory I should have coveted the senior position, but I wanted to be a Vulcan.

I grew up, went to college, earned my degree in biology, and spent twenty years working in academia, clinical research, and then corporate America being a scientist. Using logic and deductive reasoning became my mainstay for doing a good job. As I moved through each decade of my life, I became increasingly surprised at how many people just don't have as keen a need for logic as I do. For me, well, it's sort of my religion. If it's not reasonable, then it's probably not a good idea. If you cannot prove your point using sound justification that is based on verifiable and repeatable evidence, I'm probably not going to listen.

While I wish folks would use rationality more than sentimentality to make important decisions in their lives, I am able to leave room for the unexplainable. If we don't currently have the tools to measure something that could be real, then we don't have the tools. That doesn't mean something doesn't exist. I'm cool with that. But if the tools are available and you don't use them or you alter the data to support an idea that is not sustainable, I tend to have an issue with that.

When I worked in corporate America, I was responsible for taking an invention that was created in Research & Development (R&D) and transferring that small scale product to the factory. I had to make certain that it could be maintainable in large batches and sold in the market place, preferably without any failures. I worked in the Technical Product Development area. We partnered with Manufacturing and Quality Assurance to develop the process steps and the testing protocols for the new products. Then we documented those processes. It was our responsibility to create a process map for every stage of the product's movement through the factory. At times, when the procedure that we received from the scientists in R&D failed during scale-up, we'd sit down with the people who developed the prototype. It was then that we often discovered steps that were missing or inadequately defined. It was interesting, to me, to hear scientists say things like, "Well, you cannot process map everything!"

Of course you can record and verify all the steps in a process. If something exists and can be measured, it can be documented. It's often a seemingly insignificant element that can corrupt a process, once it is scaled up. Procedures can be mapped; it's just a matter of documenting the steps. Validation and testing is a way to determine the acceptable error around each step because, as we all know, nothing is perfect. That's why an over-the-counter pregnancy test states that it is 99.7% accurate and not 100% reliable. Science is about testing, measuring and logically assessing knowledge. Science has rules.

Then there's art. Art is not science. One could develop a process map for the steps that an artist takes when she creates an oil painting. That chart will be different than the one we could develop if we plotted the steps she takes to produce a water color painting or a sculpture. However, the image that she creates—that thing that comes out of her brain and only her mind—well, that cannot be mapped. That is art. Art doesn't have rules. It does not have to exist inside of process error boundaries. Art doesn't have to conform to a set of parameters. Art is the creation of imagination. It can be perfect, or even perfectly imperfect, because it is only in the eyes of the beholder anyway.

Training dogs is a lot like raising children. It exists at the intersection of science and art. There are activities which can be defined. Many of the things we do on a daily basis to keep our kids safe, to nourish them both physically and psychologically, can be documented in writing. There are about 25,000 books listed at www.amazon.com under the search "raising children". There are over 12,000 hits for the search "dog training" at the same site. Clearly, some processes can be and have been documented about raising kids and dogs. But, to me, it's obvious that one cannot raise a kid or train a dog with science, alone. There is the art which permits us to dabble in the gray area, to experiment, to utilize what is referred to a "gut feeling" or "intuition" that is nearly impossible to chronicle.

No one really knows where intuition comes from. Our

ability to perceive what is real independent of a reasoning process is truly in conflict with science. Science thrives on the need to document and reproduce events. And yet, intuition is as important to our survival as is our ability to utilize logic. In fact, one could argue that most animals rely far more heavily on intuition than reason. A lion that hunts very dangerous game must count on training and instinct along with at least some ability to rationalize or analyze the situation. Deductive reasoning (rather than just trial-and-error learning) is probably utilized by many animals, although it may not have been documented through critical experimentation in but a handful of species. One might call hunting gazelle or water buffalo an art as much as it is a science. (I wonder if lions spend much time milling over whether art or science plays a bigger role in their ability to feed their families, as they lay in the shade of a tree in the bosveld.)

As a professional who works with dogs and their people, I spend time milling over the dog-human relationship. There are many scientific studies conducted about training these days. Many dog trainers rely heavily on those reports and specifically a singular scientific model when they work with their canine subjects. My experience with dogs tells me that they are often more like us than they are dissimilar. More importantly, their behavior cannot be extracted from the relationship that they have with the humans around which they behave.

I think we know better than to assume one can use a singular scientific model for rearing children. For that reason, when attempting to resolve dog behavioral issues or teaching them new tasks, it's important that we recognize their capacity to learn through all the possible teaching models available to us and intuition, too. We need to rely on both science and art. We may need to use our heart as much as our head, but not instead of it. And, we must honor them as a unique species; morphed from a wild canine which is the primary motivator for their most basic behaviors. Dog is a species that struggles when it finds itself outside the parameters of human society and human companionship. While man had a hand in artificially selecting specific traits as dog was drawn out of the wolf, our dogs remain still a subspecies of the wolf. To ignore that fact is to fail our dogs at the very core. And, too, to disregard their complicated relationship with us, their need for our guidance and leadership, would forsake them even more. Man and dog—we are a partnership like no other.

CHAPTER 2

❧✦❧

A BIT OF HISTORY

A Man and His Dolphins

In the early 1980's, having recently graduated from college, I was employed at a University as a research assistant. The PhDs for whom I worked were conducting basic hearing research on several animal subjects, including humans and fishes. One day a man named Randy Brill signed on with my supervisor. Randy, who was the head dolphin trainer at Brookfield Zoo in Brookfield, Illinois, was pursuing an advanced degree and was interested in conducting echolocation studies with his dolphins as research subjects. He had come to our department because my supervisor had access to extensive state-of-the-art auditory instrumentation.

You know that saying about being in the right place at the right time? Well, I felt that way when Randy invited a handful of us out to the zoo to meet the dolphins. Who doesn't want to meet a dolphin? During one excursion, we were allowed to observe as the keepers conducted biannual health physicals on the marine mammals. On another occasion, I spent time playing fetch with a big boy name Nemo and his three or four buddies. I recall it feeling very much like tossing a Frisbee to a jovial, energetic puppy. In the same way that dogs interact with their people, the dolphins exchanged glances and postured in ways that we humans could understand. They also played pranks like turning the Frisbee up-side-down and flipping water at us using the flying disk as a catapult. It was all quite intentional and seemed to be inversely correlated with the amount of attention we paid to the animals. The less engaged we were, the more water was sprayed.

While on one of the private visits with the dolphins, I learned about the training method their handlers used to both create a dolphin show for the public and to manage them on a daily basis. Since you can't force a dolphin to do anything, you must have a method for reinforcing useful behaviors that they display naturally. Once the dolphin understands that you fancy a particular behavior, you can then begin to shape it into something even closer to the ultimate trick or management pose you are seeking. This might be something like accepting a swab of the vent hole for a bacteriological examination or waving a flipper at the crowd. At times the animal may be 50 feet away from the trainer when it displays a desired act, so the trainers needed a system to communicate to the dolphin that they were pleased with a specific behavior even at a distance. They created a bridge between a behavior and an ultimate reward. Without that connection too much time could elapse between the favored behavior and the ultimate reward, and the dolphin would not understand the trainer's desire to capture the behavior.

Randy and his staff used a whistle for their bridge. A toot, alone, was meaningless to a dolphin, so before they began any sort of formal training, they would introduce the significance of the whistle. This was accomplished by pairing the whistle with a food reward. First they'd blow the whistle and then toss a nice fresh mackerel. They would do this over and over again; toot—mackerel, toot—cod, toot—squid—and so on and so on. Eventually, the dolphin came to pair the sound of the whistle with compensation, which also included getting access to a favorite object or a kindhearted interaction with the trainer. From that point onwards if the dolphin were to, say, leap in the air, the trainer could blow the whistle. The dolphin was, in essence, immediately rewarded for a naturally occurring behavior. He would return to the handler for his reward, which he expected to be delivered after a whistle was blown.

A dolphin is a smart and creative thinker. After receiving an incentive, it might do a little experiment. The dolphin would perform another leap, like the one that resulted in the toot and squid response. If he again heard the whistle, he would begin to understand that leaping in the air would result in a reward. With time, if the trainers wanted the dolphin to perform the leap only at one end of the aquarium, they delivered whistles only when the dolphin performed a leap in that half of the tank. Slowly they could move the initial jump to a more specific location by compensating jumps that were closest to the desired position.

Similarly, if the handlers wanted to completely extinguish a trained behavior, they would simply refuse to blow the whistle. If the dolphin arrived awaiting a treat, he would be disappointed. Without an incentive to perform the behavior, its frequency returned to the level at which it was before training.

Finally, as the dolphin began to reliably repeat a behavior, the trainers began to associate cues (like a wave of the right hand in the upward direction) when the dolphin was most likely to perform the behavior. In this way behaviors would be paired with movements or words, and the trainers could request the animal to present a specific act. The process was as close to demanding a behavior be performed, on command, as possible.

The method was quite effective. It allowed humans to encourage wild animals to perform tricks and other more critical behaviors upon request. Without a leash or other restraining device they found they could train the wild dolphins to turn on their backs, providing access to their genitals and urinary and anal vents for examination. They taught them to accept the required handling for blood draws and dental checks. They trained them to perform sophisticated maneuvers, like synchronized jumps, object retrieving, and perhaps the most entertaining behavior of all, tail dancing.

A Woman and Her Dogs

A couple years before meeting Randy and his dolphins, I had moved to Chicago after finishing college. Within a few weeks, I had adopted an eight week old puppy. By the time I was visiting with the dolphins, through the help of folks at a dog training club which I joined, I had trained Macho through his Companion Dog (CD) title and I was working on finishing his Open Obedience (CDX) title. I had also acquired a Labrador Retriever and had earned her Canadian and American Companion Dog titles. Young, single and committed to my hobby, I had become a fairly good dog trainer by that time.

While Randy showed me schematics of the training methods they used with their dolphins, it never dawned on me that it could be employed with dogs. With two of my own in advanced levels of competitive obedience, I was fully immersed in the dog scene at the time. I had been invited to instruct the beginners' classes at my club each week. I attended fun matches and traveled to dog shows at least a few times a month. However, except for getting that familiar feeling of playing fetch while interacting with Nemo, I never compared the training methods.

With dogs we showed them what we wanted. We practiced until the dog would perform the behavior reliably. We employed communication skills that we might use to teach another human—like coaching and cheering good behaviors and correcting bad ones. It all started with the command word. Then, we could guide them physically or lure them with a piece of food. If they did something unacceptable, we could correct the unwanted behavior with a collar and leash. The idea of waiting around for the dog to sit and then whistling at them and then giving them the reward seemed like a very long way around. Dogs, after all, were domesticated to work for us, and it was pretty easy to convey our expectations. Even kids figure out how to teach their dogs to do tricks. To me it seemed as if dogs were preprogrammed to assimilate information from humans. Dolphins needed a different method.

Clicker Training

Someone finally did make the connection between the dolphin training method and dogs. Years after I had trialed several dogs in obedience and had begun to focus more on sheepdog herding, the concept of "clicker" training came into vogue. My personal life journey had removed me from the competitive obedience ring. I was raising sheep, training dogs to herd them, and competing at livestock herding events. I was teaching dog obedience classes in a building on property that I purchased just for that purpose. My classes were geared to the pet owner. I had honed my instruction skills and assimilated the techniques that best suited my style by attending numerous clinics and workshops. I paired that knowledge with the parenting skills that my own mother and father had instilled in me when I was young. In eight weeks my students were farther along and more competent than the students who graduated from a twelve-week class at my club back in Chicago.

It was through reading and conversations with some of my herding students that I learned of the "new age" approach to dog training. Yet I knew that it was really quite an old concept. It used a very similar method to the one the dolphin trainer had taught me years earlier. Instead of a whistle, a small clicking device was employed, but the concept of clicking and treating the dog was the same as whistling and tossing a mackerel. It appeared to be all the rage in the dog training world in the mid-1990s.

I remember wondering if I was going to miss out on a huge revolution in the sport of dog training while tending to the flock on my quaint little farm. At that time in addition to dog training, I was also driving 140 miles a day to get to and from a corporate job in which I developed medical diagnostic products as a professional biologist. I had long since realized that I simply could not fit more time into my life to continue competition obedience as a hobby. I had made my choice to train herding dogs, to live in the country, and teach beginner classes for the pet owner population. It meant I had to give up competitive obedience, at least at that time. On a personal level I had made the right choice, but it still left me wondering whether I might be cheating my students if I did not remain current on the latest breakthroughs in training.

And so I began to explore the clicker methods that were being touted as an evolutionary transformation in canine education. While attaining my degree in biology, I had learned about classical and operant conditioning. I had augmented my degree with several courses in psychology, some which thoroughly covered learning theories. I was quite certain that I understood the clicker training technique as it was described in the literature. It was not a new concept. Wild animal trainers had been using it with their four legged movie stars for a few decades. I did not find it impressive that dogs could be trained using the same method. If you could teach a grizzly bear to perform with the click-treat method, certainly it would be a simple task to teach a dog.

The advantage of the method, in my opinion, was most apparent when teaching animals that had little or no affinity to a human leader. They could be inspired into performing any number of activities through the use of conditioning. There was no requirement for a collar, leash, or other training tool except where personal safety was in jeopardy. The trainer needed to wait for the animal to present a behavior that closely emulated the desired final product. That was followed with the bridge sound and delivery of a reward. With progressive shaping the finished behavior could be elicited. Finally, a cue word could be added to put the behavior "on request," so to speak. But that was nothing new. I had learned that back in the early 1980's while Nemo and his pals jumped through hoops and danced on their tails.

I continued my quest to understand why the method had become such a craze in dog obedience. It did, I suspect, revitalize or help initiate sports where the dog was being asked to perform trick type behaviors. A trick, in my mind, is a behavior that has very little meaning to the dog in "dog terms." It's curious to note that the sport of Agility grew substantially during the same time that clicker training increased in popularity. Agility can be described as a series of tricks performed in sequence. Even competitive obedience can be considered a succession of tricks. Whether any behavior is a trick or an act of compliance depends upon the philosophy of the trainer and the method in which the operation is taught. If you want obedience to authority, using a food-incentive method may not help you achieve your goal.

For behaviors that are not natural for the dog, it does help to use a method that coaches them towards the end product. It is not useful to punish a dog that doesn't understand the task. A method that is based on the animal's choice to receive a treat is often more appropriate than one that requires force. I did comprehend why the click-treat method would be useful in trick training. It was clear that for trainers who did not expect absolute compliance, clicker training was a benefit. But I had been training with treats sans a clicking device for years. It just seemed simpler to use my voice as the bridge sound since I always had it with me.

When I visited the Dolphin Research Center in Marathon Island, Florida, back in 2001, I was permitted to watch training sessions up close and personal. The method was, once again the "whistle-mackerel" routine. Several times during the sessions, a dolphin simply refused to comply with the trainer's request. The trainer explained that the dolphins could not be forced to comply, so she had to be patient and simply try again. Some of the explanations that were given for refusal were the change in the weather, the fact that another dolphin was distracting the session, or that it was a new concept that the animal was learning. The notion of absolute obedience is not a possibility with dolphins. They are wild animals. One can only train to the best of one's ability and hope that, in a time of dire emergency, the animal will cooperate.

It is not because dolphins are wild animals that they can choose to ignore a cue or command from their handler. The method, regardless of animal subject, is not based on a sense of respect for authority. It's a great method for teaching any animal that responds to positive reinforcement training. Dogs, bears, chickens—it doesn't matter what species is used. Almost any animal should be able to learn using positive reinforcement training. The ultimate determination of reliability is based on how the behavior has been categorized in the animal's brain.

CHAPTER 3

꙰

THE DISCLAIMER

Before I go on I feel it is important to say that the contents of this book are my opinion based on a few decades of working with dogs and their people. I shouldn't really have to clarify that the stuff I put in my book is just my opinion. I happen to believe that is quite obvious. However, my life experience tells me that when I share an opinion some people don't like it. Often that's just because they have a different opinion. That alone is enough to not appreciate someone else's view. I understand that because I sometimes feel that way, too. Just ask my husband. Yet I've also learned that when I am quite confident in how I feel about something, I have been accused of assuming I know the truth. Confidence is often confused with conceit.

That's a sticky situation since I feel that if I have observed something enough times to have the conviction that it's probably going to happen again under the same circumstances, I do speak with great assurance. That poise or fervor can be interpreted as cockiness, I suppose. I'm sharing my own reality and that reality is real to me. I assume that is why an individual who believes otherwise would accuse me of brash over-assuredness. However, you can be secure in the idea that I have learned to add the phrases "in my opinion" or "I think" as often as I feel necessary to keep the wolves at bay. If such reminders are not offered frequently enough throughout this book for your liking, please remember to come back to this paragraph for a refresher.

I am, fundamentally, a logical and reasonable individual. My weakness would more likely be a lack of sentimentality than a deficiency in good judgment. Therefore, I expect my analyses to be questioned, and I am confident that I will be able to offer a rational response.

CHAPTER 4

❧❧

THE DOMESTICATION OF DOG

I happen to think that the most remarkable thing about domestic dog is that the species was honed by humans—morphed from the grey wolf to cohabitate with us in partnership. Although man has been able to domesticate many species of animals that provide food and facilitate travel, none compares to a dog. As a species dog is so unique, in fact, that it requires its own set of rules. A dog is not a tamed-down wild animal. Dogs possess qualities that enable them to work for and with man in a manner which is so distinctive that it is difficult to comprehend when you really think about it. Much of the time we need only look at successful ways in which we interact with other humans to understand how to interact with a dog.

I have come to believe that, like humans, dogs have an innate understanding of obedience to authority which is hard-wired into the animal because it is a social species. Dogs understand social structure and are genetically predisposed to not only desire but to need a strong social foundation in order to feel comfortable in their surroundings. To teach dogs about many of our expectations for their behavior does not require strong-arming or sugar-coating our requests. Dogs do best when they can easily identify at least one individual who they respect and who communicates with them in a way that is socially fair and just. Humans who provide sound, timely information about the ramifications of a subordinate's actions are a godsend to a dog. When that connection occurs, learning happens. The dog becomes relaxed. Everyone is happy. At least that is how I understand dogs.

Top Dog

Dogs require a leader. A dolphin in captivity requires a trainer. This singular difference sets dogs apart from all other species that interact with man. In my experience, dogs that do not have access to a good human guide often manifest a variety of behaviors that are considered "bad" by the humans that own them. Without a leader in which they can confide, many dogs attempt to take charge themselves. Others wallow in self-pity and become destructive of self or property. Still others simply tolerate the substandard conditions because dogs are wonderful at enduring our neglectful ways.

To ignore the fact that dogs are a subspecies of the grey wolf is to ignore scientific advancement. It's curious and endearing that once the technology was developed to map the DNA of an entire species, we completed the task for our own humankind first and then chose domestic dog as our second project. I suppose one could say it was a logical choice because dogs are so varied that their code could answer some very intriguing questions. I prefer to think it is because *dog rides in the jump seat of human existence*, as much today, as it did when humans first began to populate the globe.

Wolf society today is quite hierarchical, which is why many dog trainers utilize the concept of dominant-subordinate relationships to interact with and teach their dogs proper social skills. Dogs share enough DNA with their wolf ancestors that a dog can breed to a wolf and create viable young (as in puppies that, too, can reproduce when bred to another dog, another wolf, or a wolf-dog hybrid). That's a critical element in the definition of a species; if they can breed and produce viable young, they are closely related. Before DNA mapping existed, that was a well-established part of the definition of a species. Because of the relatedness of dogs to wolves, I feel that we can examine wolf behavior to better understand many of our dog's quirks. It's only fair, really, to do so. In an attempt to understand either man or dog, if we only contemplated the evolutionary changes in the species which have happened in the past few thousand years, I think we would truly be conducting a poor analysis of what motivates our behavior.

What's Pack Behavior, Anyway?

On the other hand, there are folks who study feral dog populations around the world and suggest that they mostly do not function in packs the way that wolves exist in tight family structures. They make a leap of faith and suggest that since feral dogs are not "pack animals," then we cannot use "pack structure" strategies to train or discipline our wayward pups. One could counter argue that if wolves did not hunt large game but instead scavenged for food around human garbage dumps the way that the feral dog populations do, wolves may not present with as many "pack" type behaviors either. When survival is not dependent upon each member having a keen sense of social boundaries, "pack" behavior may be less important. After all, it's a lot less dangerous to scavenge garbage at a dump than to take down a 1500 pound buffalo. However, if one simply sits and observes pet dogs interacting in a large social group or one watches a mother dog wean her litter of puppies, it's clear that warnings and physical corrections are a critical component of dog communication. The direction of that interaction is from higher ranking to lower ranking, not the other way around.

If I am going to ask a dog to learn the meaning of English words, I feel that I need to meet him in the middle when I reinforce my expectations. Dogs don't use words to communicate. It's only reasonable to try to use their method of reinforcing the message if we ask them to learn our spoken language. As a compromise, I try to emulate the way that they interact with each other when establishing boundaries for behavior. Dogs touch each other. To ignore that would be irrational. When you map a process, you can't leave out a step because you don't find it pleasant. That would not be good science.

From doing a bit of reading on the subject, I get the idea that some folks spend a lot of time refuting that dogs are "pack" animals. I think that is because they don't want to use "pack" behaviors when teaching dogs. Or, perhaps, they want to criticize people who use physical corrections by claiming that since dogs aren't "pack" animals (based on how feral dogs feed at a garbage dump), no one should use corrections to train them. Apparently, using physical corrections is considered a "pack" behavior. I think it's just dog behavior since I see dogs do it all the time. I prefer that folks who don't want to use a physical consequence based method of teaching should just say that. I would ask that they explain the rationale for their own method, rather than trying to debunk a method that they don't use.

Sales & Marketing vs. Product Development

Back in my corporate days, it was the Marketing guys who would learn about the competitor and try to explain why our product was better or why the competitor's product was worse. Those of us doing the work of creating the products didn't worry ourselves about anything except the standards that were set for the products we were developing. You can either be in Marketing or you can be in Product Development, but it's not very efficient to be in both. We in the science end of the realm did the science, generated, reviewed, critiqued the data, and provided the evidence that the product met the claims that had been set for it at the onset of the process. Sometimes, I wonder whether the "all positive reinforcement" dog trainers are more committed to sales and marketing than actually training dogs to a set standard of performance.

There remains a curious question. Should we look to wolves or feral dogs to decide how to treat our pet dogs? I think that requires an understanding of when and why behaviors developed in a species. I would speculate that Jane Goodall can sit in a city park in London or on a rock in Tanzania and see striking similarities between humans and chimpanzees regarding certain behaviors—say, the way that females nurture their babies or how an older sibling may play pranks on his kid sister. At the same time, she could see vast differences between humans and chimps. So who wins the debate as to whether it's prudent to utilize a dog-based (as in correction based) method to teach dogs or use the methods that works so well with dolphins? Read on and you will learn my opinion.

CHAPTER 5

ॐঙ৹

BUILDING BLOCKS

When I interact with clients, I begin nearly every workshop, private lesson, or class with the following sentiment: *A comprehensive canine education includes management, socialization, and training.* These three building blocks are contingent upon each other to support the rearing and daily maintenance of an enjoyable pet. To best manage your dog, you may need to implement strategies to contain him within your world and alter your environment to keep him safe. A properly socialized dog understands his position in a society, and, therefore, behaves in a respectful way towards others. As the "top dog" in the house, you are responsible to impart that information to your pup. Training is the activity of directly influencing your dog to perform tasks on command. It's both rewarding and fun to have a dog that happily executes commands, useful tasks, or entertaining tricks. Without all three of the basic elements for successful dog ownership, your dog may not develop into the enjoyable, loyal companion you hope him to be.

Management

A dog that is not properly managed can be challenging to train or may present with serious anti-social behaviors. Many dog owners error on the side of providing far more freedom than their dog can handle, rather than by being overly restricting. Insufficient management may have the worst impact on puppies. In much the same way that we offer fewer liberties to small children than we do their older siblings, reducing the chance for your puppy to get into trouble is the best policy for keeping him safe both physically and psychologically as he grows.

Using a dog crate and baby gates in the home and having a fenced yard are forms of management. A well-managed dog is supervised, confined, or controlled in an appropriate manner for the dog's age, level of training, and the situation. Young puppies require100% supervision to avoid the development of bad habits such as chewing the leg of a chair or chasing the cat. I often say that it's our job to keep a baby puppy from killing itself more than just about any other goal.

Adolescent dogs (6-12 months old) may have lost their baby teeth a few months earlier, so are no longer teething, but they maintain a high drive to explore their world. Without opposable thumbs a dog relies on his mouth to examine his environment, so he may continue to put objects in his jaws past the need to cut teeth. Once a dog has moved into mature adulthood (usually after 18-24 months), its desire to chew objects significantly decreases. If you can manage your puppy through to that stage without allowing a chewing habit to form, most dogs no longer desire to destroy things with their teeth. Supervision is the key to success.

Management also includes proper nutrition and exercise for the age and size of your dog. If you fail to provide sound management, your dog may be far more challenging than you anticipated. When you encounter a problem with your dog, ask first whether you are managing her at the level she requires. It is often easier to address a bad management issue than to resolve a behavioral problem through sophisticated training. Closing the lid of the laundry hamper is less difficult than trying to teach a four month old Golden Retriever puppy that it is unacceptable to carry a sock around the house. Nothing could be more enjoyable for a retriever than to proudly display an object filled with the scent of his favorite person. Exchanging the sock for a toy and picking up your dirty clothing may be a better solution than scolding the pup for his natural, but somewhat misdirected, talent.

Socialization

Socialization describes your dog's understanding of his position in a society. For most dogs that is the family with which they live. Deeming a dog as anti-social does not imply that he is not friendly. Your dog can be quite outgoing and yet act insubordinate at times. Many people have been bowled over by an excessively friendly dog. A well socialized dog understands that leaping on people or invading their personal space is unacceptable. In a balanced pack of canines, a lower ranking member is taught that it's not acceptable to jump on a higher ranking individual or to take or guard resources (like food or toys) from them.

When a dog believes that he can jump on people, he is acting in an anti-social manner. Young dogs learn from older dogs about proper pack etiquette, but it is your job to teach your dog proper manners when interacting with people. This usually involves providing clear, concise, meaningful consequences for unacceptable behavior. It also demands that the person who is teaching the dog remains calm, composed, and relaxed when providing the feedback about the naughty deed. Higher ranking dogs in the pack do not get angry or frustrated with their puppies. They simply provide a quick, to-the-point message that a behavior is not tolerable. Puppies often learn the lesson in one episode. If we can emulate the way that an older dog scolds a willful pup, socializing is a straightforward and reasonable experience for teacher and student. Socialization tends to be the act of shutting down unacceptable behavior.

Training

Training a well socialized, properly managed dog is a fairly simply task. A social dog has enough desire to please and respect for authority to be a willing student. Teaching a dog that is eager to learn can be very gratifying. Training is the act of pairing a cue (word or signal) with a specific behavior. Using positive reinforcement with a fair and patient approach is a good technique to teach a dog the meaning of new words. In its most basic form, training is a three step process; present a cue word, help the dog perform the task, reward.

Through training, dogs can be taught to perform

uncomplicated exercises like sit or down or highly sophisticated tasks like finding and then using a special phone to call 911 for their disabled handlers. Most dogs have a far greater capacity to learn new tasks than their owners have creativity to imagine the next skill.

Management, socialization and training are all critical, and when one is missing, often the others fail to thrive. They are the foundation for building a happy and healthy relationship with your dog.

CHAPTER 6

꒰ᔕ꒱

SOLVE THIS EQUATION

To examine different teaching approaches, let's pick one common problem and contemplate how to resolve it using various methods. Might I be as bold as to suggest the age-old issue of dog-chases-cat? The strategy to resolve a cat-chasing problem can be applied to any number of other behavioral issues. That makes it a good example.

Raining Cats and Dogs

My husband, Robert, and I have been offering a Board & Train option for wayward dogs for over a decade. During that time, I would speculate that over 80% of the dogs arrived with a desire to chase small animals. Therefore, exploring this etiquette issue is a fitting model. It's a topic that many folks may find valuable.

Prior to any method, we must establish our "product specifications," so to speak. What do we expect the dog to do and at what standard? Without establishing what we want, we cannot determine if the dog has accomplished the task or whether intervention is required. Because this is my example, I will determine the requirements. When you consider "good" behavior for your own dog, you should define the standard for "good" and share that with anyone else who may be responsible for upholding your dog's behavior.

In this example, the dog must remain sitting when a cat enters the room. He cannot get up. He cannot whine. He must not display extreme or intense focus on the cat. He must remain calm and relaxed. The cat may be permitted, perhaps even encouraged, to walk about in a typical feline promenade posture, with tail swooshing. The cat may also, if she so desires, rub against the dog. The dog must remain unruffled and permit the feline to touch him.

Since I expect the dog to display self-restraint, the handler may not use methods that restrain the dog. Tools that apply constant pressure on the face or neck are forbidden. This will include a ban on using constant, intense body posturing to hypnotize, intimidate, or coerce the dog into remaining in the sitting position. When the cat arrives, the handler may intervene briefly, if necessary, to reinforce the previously defined expectations. However, at all other times the human should be able to go about her business, comfortable in the knowledge that she is in control of the situation. The dog should be controlled by a mental rope, not a physical one.

To some, those specifications may appear very challenging. However, who wants to live with a dog that needs such constant supervision that she cannot remain calm and relaxed around her dog if there's a cat in the room? That's truly exhausting. During initial training the handler must remain on task, just like the parent of a toddler must be far more diligent than she needs to be once the kid grows up a bit. Vigilance must not be confused with tense, piercing, stiff-body intimidation. The point of the training phase is to get to the juncture in time when the dog shows self-restraint and the handler is relaxed in body **and mind— confident of the dog's behavior.**

First Attempt

Let's visualize the scenario. Only then can we fill in the gap between the dog's initial behavior and the time when his training meets the standards that we established. Here we go.

You tell your dog to sit. Because you have done some prior training, he assumes a sitting position. You smile. I remind you that you are not permitted to hold your hand up in your dog's face and chant, "sta-a-a-a-ay" over and over again while projecting your energy towards him in a way that says, "don't you dare to get up!"

He's doing a pretty good job of staying even though you want to say "sta-a-a-a-y" every now and again because you feel, at least somewhat, responsible for holding him in position with your life-force. This causes your back muscles to tighten and your breathing to become shallow. You are uncomfortable, but your dog is sitting. You are happy.

The door opens, causing a sound that piques Buster's attention. Like a princess, the cat saunters into the room, tail held high, curving just so at the tip. **She's a beauty—a deep orange tiger-striped, domestic shorthair** with four white feet and.....Oops! There goes Buster, like a rocket, directly at Miss Kitty. Wow. He's fast.

"NO! Leave It! B-u-s-t-e-r, Stop!" you shout.

Luckily, the person who let the cat in the room was in on the experiment. He left the door ajar and stood guard so that if your dog began chasing his cat, she could escape, and he could slam the door shut before your dog got a hold of her. Miss Kitty is safe, but your dog is still sniffing at the edge of the door, tail held high and quivering, whining, and, oh gosh, he's even begun to claw at the door jam a bit. Please go get your dog so that he doesn't destroy my door. Thank you.

Now, we know what Buster does when he sees a cat. He doesn't remain sitting, and even if you shout, he goes after the cat anyway. You try to argue that if I had permitted you to chant "Stay" at your dog, Buster may have remained sitting longer. You agree with me when I ask you to "be real," and I suggest that Buster would have gone after the cat even if you had been allowed to speak to him constantly.

<u>Seeking Assistance</u>

You obviously need some help with Buster, at least when it comes to his cat-chasing antics. Let's bring in a dog trainer. She is sure that she can help resolve your issues. She touts herself as someone who uses all positive reinforcement. I refer to these folks as PROP (Positive Reinforcement Only People). Her business name has the word "positive" nestled delightfully in the center of it. Her motto has the phrase "dog friendly" in bold letters. She's even certified and has attended the last three annual convention of the PROP community. She has a wrist band that connects a clicking device to her hand and a pouch containing food is strapped to her waist.

Suzie takes a bit of time teaching you how to train your dog to acknowledge the clicking device as a bridge to a reward. You use up about 65 treats establishing that connection. When you explain that your dog doesn't seem hungry any more, she warns you that you may have to withhold his meals for a while so that he only gets fed during training times. She also tells you that if your dog continues to have a low drive for typical treats, you can stuff Bugles (the extruded corn based human snacks) with liverwurst, which will keep your hands relatively clean during the training. She suggests stuffing around 100 of the crunchy cones prior to your next training class. After she shows you how to use the clicker to mark a behavior that you like, such as "sit" or "down," you explain that you really need the dog to "stay." More importantly, because you are inside this experiment contained in the book you are reading, you need to learn how to prevent your dog from chasing a cat.

"You need to learn the redirect", Suzie says.

"Yes," you exclaim. "That's what it says on the back cover of the book I'm reading!"

"To do the redirect, we'll teach the dog a word that explains that we want him to focus attention on us. Then, we'll immediately click and treat when he looks at us. We'll do this in a quiet room until he's really good at it. Then, we'll add some lower value distractions and teach Buster the redirect when, say, another dog is playing with a toy. Finally, we'll open the door and let the cat in, and we can say the redirect word and Buster will look at us, instead of the cat, and we will give him his treat".

"OK. Sounds simple," you reply.

"Yes, and it's fun, and the dog remains happy, which is

the most important part!" she replies. You think that sounds swell.

You spend some time teaching the redirect word in low distraction settings until you are very confident that Buster will turn towards you even as you begin to add a few little disruptions, like the sound of the door opening. That makes you feel very confident. If you can redirect him and give him a treat when the door opens, it should be easy for you to keep his attention when the cat strolls into the room. When you are ready, we set up the situation again. Your trainer can tell you when you will be ready to add a real cat to the training scenario. I wait patiently while you get this preliminary work done. It's common, in the all-positive-reinforcement realm, to learn that one needs to be very patient, and there's no time limit that needs to be met. I'm fine with that. Mostly.

Second Attempt

On the day that we set up the experiment again, you tell Buster to sit. He sits. You click and give him a treat. Then, we open the door—the same door where Buster has been practicing doing his redirect to the sound of the door. You smile when Buster only slightly reacts to the clatter of the door before turning his attention to you and your **Braunschweiger** Bugles. My assistant sticks his head in the door, and I nod that he can let Miss Kitty amble into the room. You have Buster under your absolute control, or so it appears.

Like a princess, Miss Kitty strolls into the room, tail held high, curving just so at the tip. **She's a beauty—a deep orange tiger striped, domestic shorthair with four white feet and...Oops! There goes Buster, like a rocket, directly at Miss Kitty. I forgot how fast that dog is!** You don't even have time to say your redirect word!

"NO! Leave It! Buster, Stop!" you shout.

Of course my assistant has permitted Miss Kitty to escape and prevents Buster from bolting after her. You tromp over to the door and gather up your dog. You seem frustrated and annoyed. You don't understand why Buster ran after the cat. He was doing so well on the redirect. His *training* had been moving along at an excellent pace.

What Went Wrong?

I believe we can explain this problem with what I refer to as Dog Algebra. The equation simply didn't balance.

When Cat = 100 and Liverwurst = 4, there's just no hope in using the redirect process. I have heard this story from dozens of my clients. The redirect procedure that they learned and practiced with a positive reinforcement trainer simply failed them.

Not only did the training fail, but you are overwrought with emotion. When you train and train and train over time, you expect the dog to do as you taught him. But, instead, he completely ignores you and chases Miss Kitty right out the door. You feel as if Buster has disrespected your authority. You are embarrassed, especially since you are in this book and everyone is going to laugh at your failure. You think Buster is being malicious. Or worse, you think he is stupid and not trainable. Yet none of those sentiments are accurate. They are just ideas in your head that can develop into really bad vibes that you project towards your dog. He knows you are disappointed, but he doesn't know why. That angers you even more. Now Buster knows that you are both disappointed and angry, and he has no way to please you.

He feels defeated.

Why doesn't the positive reinforcement method work? On paper it seems so clear. They've studied it. They did "science." How could it not solve the problem?

The math just doesn't add up. The dog wants the cat more than he wants the liverwurst. The equation is unsolvable. You are trying to solve for "O" which stands for obedience, but "O" isn't part of the calculation. There's just C for cat and L for liverwurst. You left out the O because positive reinforcement, conducted the way that you were instructed, doesn't include obedience to authority. The idea of "redirect" suggests that you can tip the scale. It relies upon sufficient training time to move to the point where the dog is so practiced at his redirect that he ignores the cat. Remember that Cat = 100 and Liverwurst = 4. They don't make sausages big enough to compensate for that inequity.

As long as the dog wants to chase the cat more than eat treats, the method is sure to fail. The technique is based on "you'll get food for behavior" rather than " do it because I said so." Sadly, some dogs suffer the emotional arrows of an owner who feels the dog should know better than to chase a cat after all that redirect training. But the method never included any component of acquiescence to a higher ranking one. How, then, is it fair for the dog's owner to expect absolute compliance? To be frustrated, angry, or disappointed in a dog that chases a cat rather than chooses a snack is unacceptable and unfair.

CHAPTER 7

૭ન્દ્ર

METHODS

My first book, 4-H Guide: Dog Training & Dog Tricks (Voyageur Press, 2009) is wholly dedicated to clearly and concisely defining three distinct methods which I use when training dogs. It is fully illustrated and offers step-by-step instruction. I think it is one of the best books on basic dog training ever written. [Please review Chapter 3 if that statement ruffles your feathers.] I am not going to repeat all of that information in this book. However, the fundamentals must be shared in order to help solve the problem of the dog-chasing-cat scenario.

1. The Social Compliance Method
2. The Incentive Method
3. The Comprehensive Method

To me, these three strategies cover all of the situations where a trainer may find herself at any stage of teaching a dog. I coined the terms myself because I did not want to confuse anyone. Some of the trainers who tout that they use exclusively positive reinforcement claim that they employ operant conditioning when they are actually referring to classical conditioning if one uses the standard text book renditions of those terms.

Confusing Terms

Some trainers use the term operant to describe only positive reinforcement techniques. Operant condition describes changes in behavior that are consequence based. The subject is in control of these behavioral changes. An example of operant conditioning would be a dog that stops barking because he receives a collar correction when he barks. Another example is a dog that sits on command because it gets a treat every time it does so. Classical conditioning results in a change in behavior of autonomic systems that the subject cannot control. A case of classical conditioning would be the ever popular Pavlov's dogs that began salivating when they heard a bell ring because the bell always preceded their meal. Salivation is outside of the dog's control.

When clicker trainers forge the connection between the clicking sound and the sensation of receiving a food reward, that's classical conditioning. They turn an insignificant cue (the clicking sound) into a very meaningful sensation (eating food), which is governed by the autonomic nervous system (not in the subject's control). Yet when you review the media that is generated by people who claim to use exclusively positive reinforcement, they seem to confuse these terms. Since there's so much perplexity regarding terminology and the complete and utter misuse of it by some of the folks in the positive-only camp, I chose to designate my own methods with words that clearly defined the processes.

Social Compliance

The Social Compliance method attempts to emulate the way that dogs communicate with one another when setting boundaries for socially acceptable behavior. This would include social expectations, such as "do not invade the personal space of a higher ranking one." In human terms that would cover don't jump on people and don't paw someone to get food. The behaviors that fall under the Social Compliance method are sometimes referred to as manners. I would like to refer to it as "socialization," because to me that is exactly what it is. However, many people have another perception of the term that includes a weekly trip to the pet supply store, regardless of whether the dog is barking and lunging at other dogs or pulling on the leash during the visit. Some people suggest that they are "socializing" their dog as it runs wildly at a dog park. If the dog is not expected to act in a socially compliant manner during those jaunts, then it's not truly socialization, in my mind.

Because it emulates the way that dogs "socialize" each other, the Social Compliance method typically requires that a negative consequence be associated with an unacceptable behavior. It establishes a respectful relationship between the dog and handler. Behaviors that can be resolved with the Social Compliance method would include pulling on the lead, nipping, incessant barking, jumping up, and chasing cats. One might consider these behaviors as being processed in the "behave properly because I said so" part of the dog's brain. I believe that it is not only my right but my responsibility to take on the role of educating the dog about what is and *what is not* acceptable and to use a method that dogs understand and use each day with each other in a well-balanced pack or family structure.

Incentive Method

The Incentive Method, which usually employs various techniques of positive reinforcement, is invaluable to teach behaviors that do not make sense to the dog from a socially compliant perspective. The dog doesn't understand that you want it to turn off the light switch since dogs don't typically do those sorts of behaviors for each other. Luring, baiting, and rewarding techniques can be incredibly useful. At times, positive reinforcement is essential to communicate the trainer's expectations. Clicker training techniques are included in the Incentive Method.

When using a reward-based technique, some people struggle as they attempt to do away with the treats. That is an important process step. After all, who wants to be required to have food around all the time to feel confident that their dog will behave properly? There are dozens of scientific papers that describe positive reinforcement methods. Many of them focus on the timing and frequency of reducing the rewards to keep the behavior intact while eliminating the food. When the dog does not continue to behave at an acceptable level once the food is eliminated, some positive-reinforcement-only trainers will blame the student for failing to follow the exact protocol for reducing the frequency and timing of the rewards.

To me, a main reason that people fail when attempting to remove the food is because they do not understand a crucial feature of the positive reinforcement method. The dog has processed the human's expectation to perform the behavior in the "I do this to get something" part of his brain, but the human is expecting him to "do it because I said so." This is a very common phenomenon. I think that the reason that humans expect the dog to behave "because I said so" is because, as social animals, that is how we tend to feel about subordinates. There. I said that word. My experience tells me that we want a lower ranking member of the pack to listen to what we have to say and honor our position whether they are kids, a coach's athletes, or someone who we hire to work for us. In that vein, we expect our dogs to be subordinate because that is the best way to control them. Most people tend to feel that it would be unacceptable for a dog to think he is higher ranking than us. That is human nature, even though the PROP may try to persuade folks to think otherwise.

When working with a killer whale, a bear, or even a dolphin, it's potentially dangerous to think that the animal is anything other than a wild animal that could kill you. Applying the ideology of social subordination makes no sense with those species. But we share our lives with dogs and sometimes even our beds with them. We trust them around our children. We can only do that by tapping into their capacity to be socially compliant. Dogs are domesticated, but, more than that, they belong to a social species that understands hierarchical order.

There is no subordination in the positive reinforcement methodology. That does not make it a bad method. It is just not the right method for certain training scenarios, including "don't chase the cat." Social species like wolves, dogs, and humans are capable of recognizing the idea that compliance is required "because a higher ranking one said so." The behavior will be reliable as long as the lower ranking one wants to be accepted as part of the pack. But as long as the animal is thinking that he is doing the behavior to acquire something valuable, he is going to wait to get that thing. Any animal will perform for incentives, but not all animals will work for an individual of authority. It is the social species that look upwards in the society to gain acceptance. We should take advantage of this aspect of our domestic dog's psychology when teaching it to work for us. To treat them like a wild dolphin is to miss the mark completely.

<u>Comprehensive Method</u>

When it is time to move skills that were trained using the Incentive Method into the social compliance part of the dog's brain, I employ the Comprehensive Method. I fully accept and embrace that some behaviors are best taught (perhaps can only be taught) using a reward based method. But unless you are simply going to consider the behavior a parlor trick that the dog can choose to perform or not perform at his whim, he needs to believe he must complete the task because you said so. If you want the behavior to be reliable at a high standard, the dog needs to shift his motivation to perform from "because I get something" to "because my mom said so." That requires a sophisticated technique which I refer to as the Comprehensive Method. You will find a thorough description of the method in my earlier book.

If you want your dog to respect you, you need to act in a way that demands respect. Using food during training can gain trust, but it doesn't earn respect. If you are going to use food in training, I believe you need to enter that workplace with a dog that has already learned to respect your authority. That way, using treats won't corrupt his opinion of your rank. After all, in most social predator species, the higher your rank, the more you get to eat. When we use food to train a dog, we need to be keenly aware of how he may perceive that undertaking.

Relinquishing a resource, such as food, can suggest that you hold a lower position in the hierarchy.

<u>Standards</u>

When I was a young kid, my parents drove us to Florida from Illinois on vacation. We stopped for lunch at a Denny's. After the meal, when we were well on our way, perhaps 15 or 20 minutes beyond the restaurant, my mother discovered that my little sister was playing with a white stone—the type one finds around landscaping. When she asked Cheryl where she got the rock, my sister said she took it from a planter at the Denny's. My mother instructed my father to turn around and go back to the restaurant, which was, of course, not what he wanted to do, but he obliged. Cheryl was required to go inside and give the rock back to the manager and apologize for taking his stone. My older sister and I were in attendance for the experience. That lesson, I'm certain, had a huge bearing on whether we chose to steal something far more valuable later in life. I consider my mother's action a way of setting a standard for behavior. If we can't steal a rock, we certainly should not take money from our mom's wallet or a pack of gum from the grocery store shelf.

The Social Compliance method begins with the idea of setting a standard for behavior. Don't bark at strangers, don't nip my pants, don't jump up, don't steal food, don't pull on the leash, don't chase the cat. Without establishing a standard, there's no way to determine whether the dog's behavior is within the specifications. I happen to believe that most dogs can uphold a level of behavior that far exceeds what their owners think is possible. There's a lot of deception when it comes to what owners imagine their dogs might be able to accomplish and also what they believe their dogs can already do.

Patience Is Not Obedience

This is worth repeating. Patience is not obedience. It is not unusual for a person to be deceived into thinking that his dog's behavior is at a very high standard when, in fact, the dog isn't really even coming close to the mark. An example of this is the most basic of exercises: the sit. I am often told by a future client that his dog already knows how to sit which implies that we don't have to work on that behavior (and sometimes implies the person wants compensation for already training that behavior!) A gentleman called because his dog was acting ferociously at the front door when people arrived. She was spitting and spinning and barking and lunging. The owner was worried that she might bite someone. "But the dog can sit and stay?" I asked.

"Yes, my dog will sit for thirty minutes," I was told.

"Well, if your dog can sit for thirty minutes, surely that's enough time to invite your guests into your house," I replied. That sort of statement usually brings an awkward silence on the other end of the line.

What I discovered through further discussion is that the dog will sit and stay for upwards of thirty minutes each night when the owner pours the food into the dish and leaves the dish on the counter. That dog will sit there, completely still, until "released" to eat her meal when it is placed on the floor. I watched a documentary on television the other night about African lions. The one lioness lay at the water's edge utterly still for eighteen hours waiting for her perfect opportunity to take down a zebra. Predators, like lions and canines, are very patient, especially if they are waiting to get something that they want. To what standard is the dog behaving? That is what we must ask. Is she behaving to the standard of exceptional patience or exceptional obedience to authority? If she were sitting out of obedience, then her owner should be able to control her at the front door when his guests arrived.

Habitual Behavior Is Not Obedience

Another area where owners often delude themselves regarding the standard of their dog's behavior is the contrast of habit versus obedience. One truly determines the temperament of a dog by asking it to do something that it doesn't want to do. I have found that most people simply never go to that place. That is why many dog owners report that their dog is unpredictable. As soon as I hear that diagnosis, I am fairly confident what will follow.

Most dogs are quite predictable. It is just a matter of who is observing the behavior whether it seems that way or not. Once you understand a few driving motivators of our companion canines, the once impulsive, unstable dog becomes quite unsurprising. Most dogs love a reliable environment. It gives them satisfaction and comfort to be able to predict what is going to happen. I would call them creatures of habit.

When a client informs me that her dog is unpredictable, it's often during a time when there is a break in the typical goings-on in the home. Each Monday through Friday, after the dog is let outdoors to potty, he receives a treat when he comes inside. The owner goes to the bathroom and finishes blow-drying her hair and then goes into the bedroom to put on her shoes. She gathers her keys and walks to the dog's crate at which time she instructs him to "Go kennel." The dog obliges as he does every weekday morning. She tosses him his cookie and leaves for work. The owner is convinced that the dog is obedient to her authority because, without fuss, each morning he goes into his crate, circles twice to the right, and plops down on the blanket that he has dug around to fit perfectly under his chin.

On Saturdays the owner sleeps in a bit late and then has a lazy morning drinking coffee and reading the paper. Dozer doesn't have to go into his crate, and he seems to understand the concept of weekends. He often gets to eat the crust of his owner's toast, something that she doesn't prepare for herself on weekdays since she stops at the drive-thru for a breakfast croissant on those days. Most Saturdays are quite different from Monday through Friday, but also most Saturdays are like all the other Saturdays.

However, last week, because her sister was getting married and she had to drive to a noontime shower, the woman told Dozer to "Go kennel," and he totally refused. He balked. He even looked like he might snap at her when she reached for his collar. She backed off and became frightened of her own dog. She is very worried. Dozer is terribly unpredictable, and now his owner is seeking assistance, but she's not sure what we can really do for him because sometimes he just completely disrespects her.

Dozer may not be as unpredictable as he is habitual. His owner has really never pushed him to see what he would do when the dog is expecting to do something else. He got the crust off the toast, so it must be Saturday. On Saturdays the crate is optional. When questioned, Dozer's owner admits that she doesn't really make Dozer do things that he doesn't want to do, and that, yes, he does really pull on the leash when she takes him for a walk, so she doesn't really take him for many walks. Dozer's owner became frightened of his behavior because she expected him to act in a typical manner in an atypical situation. Dozer behaved differently because he also felt the situation was abnormal.

There was never a relationship of respect for authority built between Dozer and his owner, at any level. They sort of worked things out. When he didn't want to do certain things, his owner simply let those things slide. She figured they were not that important. To be honest, she confesses, if Dozer doesn't want to do it, he shouldn't have to do it. That is, until she is going to be late for her sister's wedding shower.

Who's Calling the Shots?

"My dog won't let me ...." is a telltale sign of an up-side-down relationship— one which is most probably missing well defined standards for behavior. My dog won't let me trim his nails. My dog won't let me sit on this side of the couch. My dog won't let my boyfriend kiss me. Say What? Are you kidding me? These folks are not kidding me when they explain their problems. Clearly a dog that has no respect for its owner's authority is not going to appear wholly predictable. But from the outside looking in, the dog's behavior is not surprising. *Patience and habitual behaviors are not signs of a high standard of obedience to authority.*

If you want your dog to respect you, you need to act in a way that demands respect. There. I said it again. The positive reinforcement method is a very valuable technique for some training scenarios. However, it's not the best process to develop an understanding of your position in the pecking order. The idea of establishing standards for behavior is vague, if even existent, when using positive reinforcement.

If Cat = 100 and Hotdog = 4, how many sausages does it take to teach a dog to stop chasing felines?

CHAPTER 8

❧✦

POSITIVE AND NEGATIVE

I'm not going to take time in this book to provide a lengthy history about the overtaking of the dog training domain by the positive-reinforcement-only people (PROP), but it's easy to confirm. The internet is a great place to find plenty of evidence. Since the mid-1990's, media of all types have become inundated with the idea that if you are going to train a dog, you should seek a trainer who utilizes positive reinforcement techniques, *exclusively*. **It's that last word of the sentence to which I object.** To be frank, I'm not certain how the concept of exclusivity for a singular method could have become such a popular ideology because, when you really think about it, it makes no sense.

It's Been Around a Long Time

I've been utilizing positive reinforcement in training since I was a kid when I used a Milkbone biscuit to teach my miniature Schnauzer to sit and lie down. We got Caesar as a puppy in 1970 when I was ten years old. That's a long time ago. For as long, I also used corrections in training because, well, Caesar had to learn he wasn't allowed to nip us kids, and he wasn't allowed on the furniture either. That was my Dad's big rule that he demanded we follow when we debated about getting a puppy. In the end, Caesar shared the ottoman at the base of Dad's chair because that was the only furniture on which he was allowed. Well, except that he sometimes got on the orange and brown floral wing back chair just inside the living room door, but only when we weren't watching. When we returned from an outing, we kids would race inside and feel that chair to see if it was still warm from where Caesar had cheated. I digress.

It's unfortunate that the word *positive* has multiple meanings in the English language. I think that has caused quite a bit of confusion in the dog trainer's realm. Positive can simply mean a measurement in a direction opposite to that regarded as negative. But it can also suggest a movement towards progress or improvement. It can mean indisputable, unquestionable, or categorical, as in "I'm positive that limiting training to positive-reinforcement-only is not the best way to train a dog." It can suggest emphasis on what is good or laudable.

As many people know, the term positive reinforcement comes from work done by B.F. Skinner. Skinner suggested that the best way to understand behavior is to examine the causes of an action and its consequences. He coined this approach *operant conditioning.*

The concept of positive does not imply pleasant or good. Positive reinforcement means adding something that will reinforce (or increase the chances for/strengthen) a behavior. If awarding a cookie when a dog sits on command will cause the dog to sit more frequently, the cookie is said to positively reinforce the behavior.

It's easy to assume that the opposite of positive reinforcement is negative reinforcement, but that would not be accurate when using Skinnerian terms. The label "punishment" better describes the inverse of positive reinforcement. Within the confines of operant conditioning as described by B.F. Skinner, punishment weakens a behavior by the addition of something unpleasant. When a mama dog is weaning her puppies, she is apt to snap at a pup if he doesn't heed her warning (a curling lip or growl) and cease nursing. On the other hand, negative reinforcement causes a behavior to strengthen (reinforce) by the consequence of stopping or avoiding a negative experience. If going early to the cafeteria in the morning means that the yogurt flavor you love is available but arriving late means only the yucky flavors are left, you are apt to change your behavior and leave earlier in the morning for the cafeteria. To avoid the negative experience, a behavior is intensified (reinforced).

This book is not intended to be a text for operant conditioning theory. Sadly, a quick search on the internet will result in many inaccurate examples of not only the terms *operant* versus *classical* conditioning, but also the definitions of *positive* and *negative* reinforcement, punishment, and extinction. In most of my professional dog trainer life, I've tried to avoid using the terms even though I learned them back in 1979 as a college student. There seems to be at least as many misperceptions as there are accurate definitions of the terms. I don't want to get caught up in definitions. I think the words *positive* and *negative* get in the way and lead to quite a bit of misunderstanding.

Different Strokes for Different Folks

I feel that we need to recognize that there are different ways that behavior can be changed, regardless of what people choose to call the process. We can increase the chance for a behavior to happen, and we can decrease the chance for a behavior to occur. We can accomplish that by adding to or subtracting something from the dog's experience. Here are my interpretations of the basic alternatives in operant conditioning.

	Positive Reinforcement	Negative Reinforcement
"Strengthen" or Reinforce a Behavior	A behavior is strengthened by adding something pleasant (Dog gets cookie for sitting = dog sits more often)	A behavior is strengthened by the consequence of stopping or avoiding an unpleasant experience. (Leaving early for breakfast means a better choice of yogurt flavors = leaving early behavior increases)
	Positive Punishment	Extinction
"Weaken" a Behavior	A behavior is weakened by the addition of a negative stimulus (the puppy receives a nip from the mama dog during weaning = suckling behavior diminishes)	A behavior is weakened by removing a previous motivator for the behavior (Discontinue feeding the dog at the table = less "begging" behavior at the table)

With any of these methods, if the appropriate process is employed for the situation, learning can happen quickly. However, *if one tries to eliminate bad behavior with a method that rewards good behavior, failure is imminent.*

Adding A Social Component to Learning

All animals can learn when exposed to the different operant conditioning scenarios. Yet there is additional power added to the equation based on whether the animal is a social species or a loner. A rat that is placed in a Skinner Box can learn to acquire resources (hit a lever and get a morsel of food) or to avoid an unpleasant experience (hit a lever to turn off a mild electrical stimulation). A rat can even learn to respond to a light that illuminates just prior to an electrical shock by pressing the lever before the shock turns on.

An underground, electronic perimeter dog fence system hinges on this same principle. As the dog moves towards the barrier of the yard, the collar delivers a tone. It is a warning of the impending shock he will receive if he proceeds towards the perimeter boundary. Most folks report that their dog learned to avoid getting a shock after experiencing the tone + correction just a few times. The dog doesn't stay in the yard because he is obedient to his owner's authority or because he has a respectful relationship with his people. That he is a member of a social species does not increase his chances to behave better when it comes to learning to stay in his yard.

However, dogs are hardwired to be social. They have been genetically modified to do work for humans that goes beyond natural inclinations. For example, a Labrador Retriever will hunt down, retrieve, and relinquish to her owner a dead pheasant, rather than take it in the hedgerow to consume, even if she is hungry. A pack of Salukis will take down a gazelle and hold it until the humans catch up to slaughter the animal. They perform this behavior even though they have the physical capability to kill it. Because they had been on a previous hunt and had been given the entrails of a gazelle, they would understand that the gazelle is food. Yet they simply hold it rather than kill it. Bedouin hunters preferred to dispatch the gazelle under Islamic traditions, so the dogs were taught (and perhaps bred) to refrain from delivering the final blow. I find that to be an excellent example of submission to a human authority. Livestock Guardian breeds, like the Great Pyrenees or Akbash Dog, can remain unsupervised with their owner's sheep, sometimes having to hunt grasshoppers or rodents to survive, but they will not kill a newborn lamb. These examples of extreme subordination to a human's position suggest that domestic dog will go to great lengths to remain an accepted member of the pack. This awareness must not be understated.

When they denounce trainers who employ a balance of teaching approaches, the PROP rely on the fact that scientific experiments have been conducted to prove the effectiveness of positive reinforcement. Dogs, rats, chickens, goats, bears, and killer whales can all be trained with positive reinforcement. Remarkably, all animals can also all learn via the other processes defined in operant conditioning, including positive punishment. Electric fencing is often used to contain wild animals in zoo enclosures. Which process one chooses to change an animal's behavior must take into consideration a number of variables.

I think it's imperative to recognize that dogs evolved shoulder-to-shoulder with man. Some people embrace the notion that wolves tamed themselves into domestic dog by scavenging the large garbage pits that man created once he cultivated a more stationary lifestyle. Others envision cavemen stealing baby wolves from a den and taking on the artificial selection of the species from its most raw state.

Regardless of how it happened, it's hard to refute that dogs developed next to man, and man developed next to dogs, perhaps even because of dogs. This social bond cannot be understated.

Positive reinforcement is an important and valuable method of teaching animals, including our own children. However, relying upon it exclusively, to train a dog is illogical. Using the "because I said so" part of a dog's brain to achieve expectations for behavior is not only judicious, but essential, especially since an anti-social dog will often use his teeth to control his situation. To neglect this principle is to fail to honor dog as the unique species that it is.

So if Cat = 100, we need to tip the scale in our favor. I suggest that we do that by tapping into our dog's innate desire to become a socially accepted member of our pack. Once we establish ourselves as a higher ranking individual, we can plug into that system quite easily. As long as we treat our dog as just another wild animal without regard for the uniqueness of his species, we will be as successful at training dogs as dolphins. Ask any honest dolphin trainer if she can completely rely upon an exclusively positive reinforcement method to control her charges, and you may be persuaded to consider what I am about to share.

CHAPTER 9

❧❧

WHICH STRATEGY?

Positive Reinforcement?

Let's get back to Buster and Miss Kitty and contemplate our options. Why does positive reinforcement fail to teach Buster to ignore a cat? Positive reinforcement is designed to strengthen a behavior through the addition of a reward. We want to eliminate a bad behavior (chasing) not strengthen a good behavior. However if you have as an agenda the exclusive use of positive reinforcement, then you can only reinforce good behaviors as a way of teaching. Yet, as Buster's owner you hope to eliminate the cat chasing behavior. Again things just don't add up.

Since the PROP are opposed to any method other than positive reinforcement, they need to get creative with their approach. What can we positively reinforce in this canine vs. feline situation? Their solution to the problem is to suggest that a dog which is focused on his handler cannot also be chasing a cat. If they teach the dog to focus on a person when a cat comes around, they can continue to use a positive reinforcement-only method.

Unfortunately, redirecting a dog from something he considers very valuable requires a prize that is even bigger than his original objective. I speculate that we could create the Oscar Meyer Weiner Mobile completely out of bologna, and a dog that wants to chase a cat isn't going to care. To augment the unreasonable approach of using positive reinforcement to stop unwanted behavior, PROP trainers suggest that it may take a very long time, and it will demand that your timing be exceptional and your commitment to the process be top notch. You should start out with the cat very far away so that it isn't much of a motivator of bad behavior. When Buster responds to your redirect word and eats the treat most of the time while the cat is 80 feet away, you can move the cat a bit closer. In time you should be able to habituate Buster to accept the cat. Sometimes this is called desensitization. You may have to continue feeding him treats to support this *good* behavior because extinction will occur if a behavior isn't being reinforced frequently enough. Ugh!

Not only does that sound challenging, but hidden between the lines is a little leap of faith that you are expected to take. If Buster gets rewarded for "good" behavior, as in focusing on the handler when there's a cat around, then he is somehow going to assimilate the lesson that chasing the cat is "bad," even though the training never really addressed that menace. It simply doesn't work that way. Try it.

Here's one of those instances when I am going to make a claim that others may simply refute and say, "yes it does work," to which I would reply, "show me." Based on my experience, redirecting a dog's focus away from a highly rousing object (like a cat) towards a food lure does not teach a dog that chasing cats is not acceptable. I have met a few cat obsessive dogs in my life and, believe me, their obsession often doesn't go away over time no matter how much time passes and whether or not Bobby Flay provides the food that is offered during the redirect training. The method has been described on dozens (maybe hundreds) of websites, on TV, and in books. If you look closely, most of the descriptions are copycat versions of another post from a different site. It is as if someone once described the protocol and then everyone just repeated it until folks decided it must be real and truthful. Saying something over and over again doesn't make it accurate. **The redirect protocol doesn't work**. That's my opinion and this is my book and I'm going to share my opinion openly.

When Cat = 100 and Hotdog = 4, you best have a tight hold on the dog or Miss Kitty is going to use up one of her nine lives fairly quickly around a dog like Buster. And did I mention, it is quite bothersome to keep a piece of food around in the event that a cat shows up, especially if your dog requires liverwurst stuffed Bugles? Remember, extinction of a positively reinforced behavior will occur if the action isn't reinforced with some regularity.

Extinction?

I think I have made my point that ending cat-chasing behavior with a method designed to create desired behavior isn't prudent. So what do I propose instead? Let's consider the options. Perchance it would be fruitful to ask ourselves why Buster is chasing the cat. There may be a chance that we could employ extinction to our advantage. Contemplate a wolf pup that is just learning about hunting.

On some days one of his parents brings home a live rabbit. Poor bunny is stunned from the experience and is acting more like an opossum than the lagomorph that it is. Mama wolf presents the rabbit to her pups. The pups begin sniffing and nudging it with their noses. When the bunny thinks she has a chance, she takes off in a serpentine escape pattern that causes the pups to take chase. Eventually one of the juvenile wolves gets ahold of the hare and delivers the final blow. The three pups devour the little meal. Chasing rabbit behavior becomes reinforced.

A week later the wolf pups encounter a large flock of geese on the edge of a lake. The scent of goose is familiar to them because a few weeks ago, when the geese were molting and unable to fly, the mama wolf brought one home for dinner. The pups freeze, stalk, and approach within ten yards before the big birds take flight. For a few days they try their paws at hunting geese again. Each time the potentially delicious birds escape. Chasing-geese behavior extinguishes.

If Buster is pursuing the cat for the soul purpose of catching and eating Miss Kitty, maybe we could extinguish the previously rewarded behavior. If we could set up a scenario where Buster's behavior did not yield his expectations we may be able to eliminate his drive to chase cats. Dealing with each problem on a case by case basis is admirable so I would suggest that we determine whether we could solve the problem that way. However, it would require putting a few felines in danger while Buster learned that he will never get his prize, so I'm not sure it's the best choice. I also suspect that, except in very rare cases (and I will share one later in this book), cat-chasing behavior is not exclusively motivated by the need for nourishment.

I acquired my first Border Collie in the late 1980's. I've trained and trialed no less than a dozen of them in herding competitions, and I've owned nearly twice that number. I've also given herding lessons to dozens of dogs of various breeds. I understand herding behavior is an instinct that was cultivated out of natural behaviors of wild canines. In its most simple form herding is a dog's desire to contain and control prey.

In recent years some people have utilized the Border Collie's heritable traits to tackle the overabundance of Canada Geese on golf courses, air strips, and around the ponds of industrial parks. Since the wild geese are able to fly away, the goose patrolling Border Collies never achieve the satisfaction of truly containing their charges. Because of my experience working with livestock herding dogs, I have always thought it would be terribly frustrating for the dogs when their subjects simply flew away since the innate desire would never be rewarded. But the Goose Dog handlers report that their dogs continue to work even though they never reach the true aspirations of a herding dog: to contain and control. Instead, they simply drive off the birds and move onto another opportunity to do the same.

If Buster's cat chasing behavior is part of his inherited canine yearnings to hunt down game I would like to boldly suggest that waiting for it to extinguish by using a method of prohibiting him from ultimately catching Miss Kitty will be hugely unsuccessful. Positive reinforcement and extinction are now scratched off our list of methods we can effectively employ to resolve Buster's naughty behavior.

Negative Reinforcement?

Well then, what about that oft confused process referred to as negative reinforcement? *Oh, no, not* negative. *I don't want my dog to experience anything negative!* Don't worry. It doesn't apply to our problem. Negative reinforcement defines a scenario where a behavior is strengthened (reinforced) when we remove an unpleasant experience. Remember, negative reinforcement describes why you begin to leave home earlier every morning to gain access to a better selection of yogurt flavors at the cafeteria. A canine example might be a dog that has been taught to lie down on command, but does so very slowly or sometimes refuses. If we create an unpleasant experience that he can escape by lying down we will be using negative reinforcement. Applying downwards tension on the dog's collar and releasing that uncomfortable feeling as soon as his elbows reach the ground would be an example of negative reinforcement assuming that the dog learns to lie down more quickly to avoid the tension on his collar.

Negative reinforcement hinges on strengthening a behavior. For the same reason that positive reinforcement isn't appropriate, negative reinforcement is not going to help us eliminate Buster's pursuit of kitties. We want Buster to cease chasing not begin to do something else instead.

CHAPTER 10

෨෬

THE POSITIVE SOLUTION

Curiously, we are left with a "positive" option to resolve Buster's problem. According to B. F. Skinner, positive punishment is the addition of an aversive to reduce the frequency of a behavior. It is a scientifically proven process. I find it peculiar how often the PROP suggest that the reason positive reinforcement works is because there is scientific proof that it does. Well, there's scientific proof that negative reinforcement, positive punishment, and extinction work to alter behavior as well.

What Is Better?

I have come across many claims that positive reinforcement is the preferred method because it works *better,* or *best.* That begs the question whether the people who utilize an exclusively-positive-reinforcement approach to training actually understand the differences between the unique processes of operant conditioning. Since we've already identified that positive reinforcement will strengthen a behavior and positive punishment is designed to eliminate behavior, how can one be better than the other? That's like asking whether an orange or rice is better. I guess it depends upon whether you are making a savory or a sweet dish. If you want to eliminate cat-chasing behavior it would be prudent to select a method that is designed to weaken a behavior. If you want to create a behavior it would be reasonable to select a method that is designed to strengthen a behavior. Positive reinforcement is the better method to encourage experimentation. However, we don't want Buster to experiment with Miss Kitty.

When I want to teach a prospective Service Dog to perform tasks like "turn off the light switch", "pull off my socks", or "fetch that item" I need to immediately compensate behaviors that are at least somewhat close to the final standard. In the initial lessons, I find it acceptable if the dog doesn't truly turn off the switch. If he puts his paw anywhere close to the switch, I will reward him. I want him to feel free to experiment. I want to encourage him to explore his options for gaining the reward. I hope that he presents something close to the final behavior, but I don't wait to deliver a reward until he has it down pat. If I did that, the dog would quit trying. Positive reinforcement is the better method for creating new behaviors especially those that make little sense to the dog from a social compliance perspective.

When I want to teach a prospective Service Dog to refrain from alerting to or chasing squirrels, I need to discourage experimentation. I cannot be ambiguous. I must be clear every time, and consistent in my message: don't chase squirrels. I must set a standard and reinforce that specification. I must be willing to impose my will on the dog and do so well before the actual unacceptable behavior is presented. I want the dog to learn that I can read his mind. I can see that he is thinking about chasing and I must warn him prior to the act. Then my intervention can be fairly minimal but effective to keep the dog's attitude in the right place.

In the morning I can use the Incentive Method to teach the dog to turn on a light switch, and I can work on Social Compliance behavior in the afternoon of the same day. The methods are mutually exclusive, and dogs understand both principles simultaneously. I have not found that it is confusing for a dog to shift between learning styles depending upon the situation.

Because the dog training realm can be so confusing-with "professional" and "certified" individuals misrepresenting or confusing the "science" that they hold so dear, when I wrote my first book on training, I coined the terms Social Compliance Method and Incentive Method because it just makes things so much simpler. The Incentive Method is just that: a process in which the dog learns because he is offered an incentive for his behavior. Most often the incentive is food but it could also be access to a favorite toy or even playing a unique game with the handler.

Positively Social

The Social Compliance method is not simply Skinner's definition of positive punishment. It is rooted in the fact that we are working with dogs—and not dolphins, not chickens and not bears. If you use an underground electronic fence system, your dog remains on your property because he has learned that moving towards the boundary will result in a tone which is immediately followed by a shock. He can avoid the shock by changing course when he hears the tone. He assimilated that important lesson through the process of positive punishment. His unacceptable movement towards the perimeter results in the addition of a negative experience. However, as I explained earlier he is not staying in your yard because he has any sort of respect for your authority.

The term Social Compliance does not only encompass the idea that a dog will receive a correction for an unacceptable act. There is more (and less) to it. The reason that it's more complicated is because dogs are not dolphins. They are a unique species that should be honored and managed differently than just any ol' animal. They are born social—not just social within their own species (like dolphins may be) but they come equipped to be social with humans, too. That's weird, but it's true. The PROP's failure to recognize this point is in conflict with the idea that an all-positive-reinforcement method is dog-friendly. How can something be dog-friendly when it completely misses the mark regarding the basic understanding of what it means to be a dog?

I have had the pleasure and responsibility of raising a number of litters of puppies. It is truly impressive how in eight short weeks those little animals move from helpless, blind, deaf, nipple-seeking-missiles that cannot even regulate their own temperature to competent little doggies that can go off with a different owner and adjust to a new life almost effortlessly. What I find even more remarkable is how, at just four weeks old, they are seeking out a relationship with me— a human. It's not necessary to tame baby puppies. They come that way. They want to interact with people. They look you right in the eyes. They trust. They submit. They accept, not just tolerate, that their life includes having a relationship with another species.

The Human-Dog Bond

If you are reading this book I suspect you have a dog. Maybe it's even a terribly unruly beast that makes your life miserable much of the time. But I also speculate that you've had a few of those magical moments with your pup. You've felt that extraordinary connection, that kinship, the sense of partnership and loyalty that can only be realized between humans and dogs. There is no other inter-species association that rivals the one between man and dog. Dogs take us with all our flaws. They forgive us for all our bad-tempered spells and they accept us even in our most ugly moments.

We can, in fact, parent our dogs like we do our children—apply the cleverness of conversation rather than the cold, hard science of learning theory. But we must parent them like we do our children rather than spoil them like our grandchildren. That means we are obligated to develop trust and respect with our dogs. We must work at maintaining that rapport, understanding, and reverence for our position. We must recognize our responsibility for their welfare and development. *To seek friendship before deference has potentially lethal ramifications.* We must develop such an art form, relying upon knowledge of those who came before us and our own capacity to make appropriate decisions, sometimes in an instant, based on reasonable and logical principles and sometimes using gut feelings.

Just as we can take advantage of some very basic elements which are hardwired into social species when raising our children, we can exploit those qualities in dogs. The young of social species seek out relationships with their elders. There appears to be a keen understanding that survival depends upon those connections. Parenting requires that we instill a wee amount of fear in our children. I happen to think that puppies come with a natural concern about being rejected from the pack. For that reason they do not want to disappoint. They cannot survive if they are banished for bad behavior. It is that same sort of fear of disappointing a parent (at least until adolescence arrives) that grants human mothers and fathers a level of control which could not exist if the children did not have such natural apprehension. That phenomenon exists in dogs as well.

Respecting Boundaries *in absentia*

I was at our county fair a few years ago watching my 4-H students show their dogs. It's a quaint event in a small, rural community. When the dog show was over a handful of ten year old little girls grouped together giggling and contemplating what they would do next. It was a beautiful summer evening. Having moved through and beyond the stress of competing with their dogs, they seemed wholly unencumbered. A few minutes earlier I had seen their parents handing out a few dollars to each child—money which they were being given to enjoy some of the amusements that the fair offered. One little girl said, "Do you wanna go ride the roller coaster?" to which her friend replied, "Naw, my mom won't let me."

I sat in wonderment. Clearly, at ten years old the girls could have snuck away and enjoyed the ride. Their parents had granted them permission to leave the umbrella of their authority while they stayed behind with younger siblings to watch the bunnies being judged. Yet part of parenting is the development of "because I said so" control over the kids even when the parents are out of sight. It is exceptional practice for becoming an autonomous and responsible adult. Learning to respect societal boundaries even when there isn't a policeman watching your every move is part of being social. Fortunately, at least in my opinion, social species come equipped to assimilate those lessons. Respect for authority, even *in absentia*, is a critical attribute of a dog or a human that exists with and relies on others.

When a pup is very young many adult dogs will tolerate its somewhat anti-social behavior. For example, to enter the personal space of a higher ranking one is considered unacceptable for most dogs. But baby puppies are often permitted to climb on or over an adult or tug on an ear or tail. However, there comes a day of reckoning when what was permitted yesterday is corrected today. A vital step in the communication process between senior dog and the less informed is the addition of a warning signal that almost always precedes the delivery of a negative consequence. A curled lip, a low growl, pinning back of the ears, or a shift in the tail set can all inform a lower ranking dog that he's about to breach a boundary.

Getting Physical

A common criticism from the PROP is that a physical correction is cruel. My methods are rooted in helping a dog move from an anti-social to social state of existence. That is the definition of the Social Compliance method. Often, a dog has become anti-social because no one in its life ever took control and set clear standards for the dog's conduct.

In my opinion, giving a dog food for good behavior does not help explain to the dog about unacceptable behavior. That leaves the dog wanting more information. If you don't tell a dog what is right and also what is wrong, he cannot ever truly behave how you expect. It leaves the dog unable to satisfy you. Domestic dog is hard-wired to try to please a human leader. To prevent that actualization is cruel.

I observed a parent teach her infant to remain in a highchair during dinner. The first two, three, four, perhaps five times that the child tried to climb out, the parent "touched" the child by placing him back in the chair. She did this without emotion (no frustration, no anger, no disappointment). At times the child protested by whining, crying, or having a tantrum. I did not consider his campaign as confirmation of parental abuse. It was evidence of the child's protest, nothing more.

By the sixth attempt, when the child began to climb out of the highchair, the mother began to stand and the child sat back down. A good parent will not harm her own child when teaching him to remain seated in the chair. However, she may have to touch him to give him feedback that she does, in fact, control his destiny and she will impose her will upon him. To ignore this duty could result in an injured child (and an abysmal teenager).

Of course there are times when the parent praises the child for doing a good job. She could even praise him for staying put in the chair, but if he begins to climb out, praise won't keep him in the chair. A consequence for non-compliance is needed. That is how the mind of a social primate (and social canine) works. It is based on establishing a social order. Mother trumps child. Full stop.

There are times when a parent may need to physically control the child for its own safety and to teach it about boundaries. That physical touch is important since a small child doesn't have the capacity to completely follow verbal directions yet. Curiously, the way that we groom a child to follow verbal instructions is by touching them when they are little. They learn that we can and we will touch them. Then they heed the verbal warning and comply so as to avoid the physical touch. The touch is not painful. It is clear information that if the child doesn't heed the verbal request the parent will simply control the child physically.

Dogs do the same thing with their puppies and lower ranking adults. They just happen to do it with their teeth since they don't have access to their "hands". They touch a pup if it doesn't heed the initial warning (such as, "don't come near my rawhide bone"). They make contact around the neck or face. That is why it is tradition to use a collar when interacting with a dog regarding standards for its behavior. A senior dog doesn't intend to damage its junior pack member. However, the interaction has to be meaningful enough to leave an impact.

I was at a city park a while ago. In a nearby parking lot a man stood next to the open door of his mini-van. His toddler was bent over near the front of the vehicle grabbing at pebbles in a pool of water that remained from the prior day's rain. When the man finished organizing his parcels, he turned his attention to his daughter.

"Madeline!" he shouted. The child showed no response.

"Madeline, come here," he proclaimed. Madeline remained fixated on the little stones.

"Madeline!", the father repeated. Nothing.

"Madeline, let's go," he said for the fourth time.

I turned to my husband and said, "When that child turns thirteen, that guy is going to be in a heap of trouble." Robert smiled.

Say It Once – Make It Happen

What do I think would have been a better strategy to teach Madeline to listen to her father's directions? Without shouting or projecting any negative emotion, I suggest Madeline's father should have simply said, "Madeline, come here, please." If there was no response, he should have walked the four feet from the open car door to the child. He should have lifted her into his arms or taken her by the hand, walked back to the car door, and put her into her car seat— no anger, no frustration, no disappointment. Just teaching a standard.

I would follow the same basic process when working with a dog. Essentially, the method is "say it once, then make it happen." The reason that people become frustrated and angry is because their expectations have not been met. Rather than recognizing that they truly do have power over the situation, rather than making it happen in a calm and deliberate manner, they get irritated and repeat the demand, usually with an edge to their tone and increase in volume, too. I would suggest that the dog did not respond because it did not understand the person's expectations.

Interestingly, I think that both dogs and people prefer to believe they have free-will to do as they please. Both canine and human would rather be self-restrained than restrained. When we use a method that provides clear information about our expectations, both dogs and kids often begin to comply to our verbal requests quite quickly. This is especially true when they believe that we will "touch" them if they do not respond. That touch cannot be made in anger. Once puppies and kids learn how they can push our emotional buttons, they win. The most critical aspect of using a method of "say it – make it happen" is to remain calm, confident, and competent in the delivery. Once we permit ourselves to become frantic, frustrated, or furious, we have lost the battle.

Although the PROP often suggest that a significant benefit of an exclusively positive reinforcement method is the lack of contact between handler and dog, it is not abusive to physically manipulate a dog in order to teach a valuable lesson about survival. It is useful in parenting small children and it is good dog ownership. If you think a child can be "clicker trained" to remain in a high chair without falling out first, might I suggest that you try it with your own kid. Like humans, dogs touch each other. They understand that method. To use physical touch in training is natural and beneficial.

When teaching, one must enter the relationship with the proper attitude—calm, confident, deliberate clarity regarding the message about the dog's behavior. Sometimes it requires physical contact. When it is done properly, it has long lasting, positive effects on behavior. It is also the closest technique to the way that dogs interact with each other.

CHAPTER 11

୬~ତ

IT'S ONLY NATURAL

Observation is an important scientific method in ethology (the study of natural animal behavior). I truly enjoy watching dogs interacting with one another. Of noteworthy mention is that I rarely see dogs utilizing an incentive based method with each other. I have not been privy to Sadie communing with Bailey, "Hey, Bailey, come over here and help me dig this hole and I'll share my food with you!" I have never seen dogs use incentives to establish boundaries for behavior. "Hey, Bailey, if you don't jump on me, I will give you my tennis ball." It just doesn't happen.

I do think that when dogs encourage each other to play there's an element of enticement. Both dogs benefit from the chase or playing tug-o-war or even rolling around and "mouth wrestling" (that odd interaction where two dogs will bite on each other around the neck and mouth area which is often accompanied by aggressive sounding vocalizations). But those dogs are typically of fairly equal status in the group. It is far less common to see a high ranking dog mouth wrestling with a much lower ranking pup. Senior dogs do not use incentives to set boundaries for acceptable, social behavior. Instead, they display a warning and then deliver a physical correction if the junior dog doesn't heed the caution and change course. There is a hierarchy, and the dogs tend to respect it. I don't think it's sensible for a human to assume an equal-status role with a dog. It is confusing, and it can be dangerous to permit a dog to believe he can put his teeth on you, yank a toy from your grasp or pull you around on the leash.

Humans Find It Natural, Too

Our own human society is also built on the premise of social compliance. We rarely use incentives as a way to control our citizens' behavior. In a free society you may establish a way to gain incentives as long as you are not breaking any established rules. If you are good at making pizza and you want to sell it at your shop, then you can make money selling your savory pies. The folks in your community will also be rewarded because there's a good pizza place where they can eat. If you would rather earn money by fixing motorcycles then, you can do that. However, on your way to work regardless of whether you are going to your pizza place or your cycle shop, we don't want you to speed while driving. We consider that a danger to others in our society.

In general, as a community we determine and then document what we consider unacceptable behavior. We spend less time sizing up what is acceptable since that list could be very long, and we may never complete it. We focus on what we consider objectionable. We establish fair, negative consequences for misconduct, and then we determine how we are going to judge and enforce the law.

As an example, take speeding while driving. The law states that the top speed limit on Interstate 94 is 65 miles per hour. We document that in the written law. We post it for the citizens to view. We decide that when a driver exceeds 20 mph over that posted limit, the fine will be $140. We hope that price will be a deterrent to future speeding. If speeding doesn't decrease, we may review the potency of our consequence and increases that fee to $180. A typical objective of imposing fines for unacceptable behavior is to improve future conduct. Cynics would argue that it's also a way for the state to earn revenue, and, to be honest, I can't really argue with that point. However, that's a fringe benefit of the system that still delivers the unpleasant ramification for speeding on our public roads.

As long as he drives at the posted speed limit, we enjoy having the pizza guy in our society. We like his rendition of "the everything pie" minus the green pepper because, well, I just don't like green pepper on my pizza. As a society we attempt to balance the punishment to the crime. $140 for 20 over seems fair and effective. However, with some of the most heinous offenses, we banish the individual from our society. Dogs do the same thing.

Dogs Enforce Social Compliance

Typically, dogs that exist in a balanced pack want to welcome and tolerate any other dog that enters the group. They post their rules using visual or auditory warnings in much the say way that we post speed limit signs. They deliver the ticket swiftly and effectively for the specific crime. But on occasion a dog's behavior is so far outside of social tolerances that he is banned from the pack. This can be through death or simply chasing him off (sort of like human society). When a rogue individual threatens the tranquility of the family structure, action must be taken. The take-home message of this commentary is that **dogs don't use incentives to teach other dogs what is acceptable behavior**. Dogs establish social compliance through warnings and consequences. While human society is far more complicated, it is mostly based on the same basic premise.

My next book is dedicated to exploring a few principle tenets that I believe dogs utilize to remain socially balanced and how we humans can learn some really important lessons from our dogs in that regard. I'm not going to say much more here other than that dogs need to be social. It is a core part of their make-up. They are driven to foster and grow a healthy relationship with a higher ranking individual that they trust and respect. I believe that humans use very similar strategies to survive even in the concrete jungle that many of us now call home.

Don't Forget the Jam and Butter

In my experience, employing B. F. Skinner's positive punishment model alone is not as effective as also tapping into a dog's need to be part of the family—part of a pack, part of a social unit. Being an affiliate of the collective is a necessity for individuals of a social species. To ignore this concept is like eating toast without butter and jam. Bread alone can nourish you, but it's the butter and jam that enhances the experience and adds many levels of complexity to the pallet. The process of Social Compliance includes the use of positive punishment. However, the intensity and the frequency of corrections required can be significantly reduced when the subject comes with a good dose of desire to please, respect and loyalty.

The gaze that a human mother exercises to get her son

back into alignment, in its purest sense, could be considered a simple cue to an impending correction. Just like a dog will change course when his wireless-fence collar beeps, Tommy may choose to change his behavior when he sees the image of his mother's glare. The process can be accomplished in a Skinner Box with a rat, a lever, a light and an electrified grid, but it's hard to refute there's a force associated with the mother's scowl which is more potent than the simple positive punishment model describes.

I believe that extra effectiveness comes from the mother's deeply rooted need and her confidence that she can and will impose her will on the child. That power is paired with Tommy's need to remain in good stead with the one person he can rely upon to keep him safe. Tommy is not permitted to hit his baby sister, and his mother will make certain that he learns that lesson. The influence that is associated with that "look" is something akin to Kung Fu. Martial arts describes "breaking bricks with one's fist" as a speed, time, impulse physics sort of thing. However, even if you form your hand properly and stand with the correct posture before delivering the blow, if you have any doubt, you won't break the bricks. (You may break a few of your fingers while trying.) Like the Kung Fu master, if the mother believes that she can control Tommy's behavior, she will.

The capacity to influence another being is directly proportional to the belief that you can. I am convinced that is a law of nature even if it has not been quantified. Maybe that's because we don't have the proper measurement tools yet. When we train dogs, we must have no fear that we can in fact influence the dog. If that presence of mind is missing, then the dog will learn to walk all over us. It doesn't matter how you hold the leash, how hard you tug on the collar, or even what sort of collar, harness or halter you use. Command comes from the belief that you deserve such power over another entity. Dogs and humans alike respond to such influence.

This may not be true if you are trying to control a dolphin, a bear or a bobcat, but those are wild species that don't come with the hardwiring that dogs and humans have. The reason that we can control dogs is because at a cellular level they are aching to be controlled by a higher ranking individual that knows what is best for their survival and who will take the helm and lead.

The Measurable Process

Passion and desire to lead is not sufficient to control a dog. There are process steps that must remain intact. For example, without consistency learning doesn't take place no matter how calm you might be when dealing with the dog. One must be consistent when delivering the information. Predictability and reliability are qualities of a good instructor. Proper timing is important. Responding proactively to an impending behavior will have a huge influence on how triumphant a trainer will be. However, if one's energy is off, if there is frustration, fear, anxiety, anger or disappointment associated with the delivery, then there's a chance the dog will not even experience the information you are trying to impart.

I refer to this phenomenon as the "art" of training. Science can take us only so far. Remember, we can map the process that an artist takes to create an oil painting, but we cannot articulate the method that gives rise to the actual work of art. We cannot capture and sell the product called "good energy," which, when applied during training, has a monumental influence over whether a pup learns or not.   We can only show the effects of its labor and encourage others to emulate it.

CHAPTER 12

༺∝ঙ

REACHING THRESHOLD

Let's get back to Buster, Miss Kitty, and algebra. After all you probably picked up this book because it promised to help you solve a dog training problem using a method other than the positive reinforcement techniques which have not been working for you. To recap—we have a dog named Buster who has a cat chasing problem. If we were to apply a value to how desperately he wants to chase cats, we'd score his behavior at 100 units.

The positive reinforcement method that our first trainer suggested stipulates that we redirect Buster's attention away from the cat whenever it approaches. To accomplish this we taught Buster to look towards us when we uttered a verbal command. We achieved this by offering a food reward whenever he looked at us. We were told that when the cat visited, we could say the cue word to redirect Buster's focus from the cat back to us. Our instructor said that the positive reinforcement method is the scientifically better technique to train our dog.

Unfortunately, we don't really care if Buster looks at us when we give him the cue word for the redirect behavior. We care that Buster doesn't chase the cat once he sees it again. We are fairly certain Buster will see the cat again because he has pretty good eye sight. More importantly, that dog has one heck of a nose. Buster can smell Miss Kitty coming before he even sees her! That puts us, as his teachers, behind the eight ball since we cannot always proactively redirect Buster.

Another problem that we have encountered is that the highest value treat that we can find—that reward which Buster just loves more than any other treat—only scores a measly 4 on the scale of what motivates Buster. When cat = 100 and liverwurst = 4, the math doesn't add up. The equation doesn't balance. Buster will continue to chase the cat. He wants to chase the cat 96 motivational units more than he wants to eat liverwurst. That's a lot of motivational units that Buster begins to aim towards Miss Kitty before we even know she is coming. It just seems so overwhelming that, to be honest, many dog owners would report it is impossible to resolve. But I know a method that will work.

The approach doesn't alter the value of liverwurst. It's still Buster's favorite treat, and it is still only worth 4 motivational units. However, this process may have an influence on the absolute value that Buster places on cats because he will discover a force greater than feline magnetism. It is driven by a desire that may trump hunting as an individual. It is his need to be social.

We aren't going to use positive reinforcement to attempt to diminish Buster's cat chasing response because, according to the person who coined the term positive reinforcement, the method isn't applicable to situations where we want the subject's response to subside. We are going to use a method that has been scientifically documented to weaken a response which, when you think about it, is the logical choice. Why use a method that creates good behavior when we want to reduce bad behavior?

To Correct Is to Fix

In the operant conditioning realm the technique is called punishment. Positive punishment is a correction based method. The word punishment tends to conjure up many different images in people's minds. Some people think that a "time out" is punishment. Some people think that punishment involves taking away toys or other pleasurable objects. Others think that spanking is punishment. So, which is it? What sort of punishment should we employ to fix Buster's cat chasing problem?

Let's focus on the specifics. We want to fix a problem. According to operant conditioning theory, applying a negative response to an unwanted behavior will lead to the reduction of that action. The negative response is called a correction. To correct means to fix. We need to correct Buster for chasing cats, and the cat-chasing behavior will diminish. Therefore, we will fix the problem. Based on a couple of decades of working with dogs and their people, I know that the concept of a correction is one of the most misunderstood principles in dog training.

When Corrections Don't Work

Here's a common phenomenon. A potential client calls

me complaining that her dog is pulling on the leash. She asks what I suggest that she do to resolve the problem. I propose that she corrects her dog for pulling.

She claims, "that doesn't work."

I ask, "what doesn't work?"

She responds, "Correcting the dog doesn't work." She says that she has been correcting him for a long time without resolution.

I ask, "how long have you been correcting the dog?"

She says, "it's been six years."

I inform her that she has probably been nagging her dog but that she has not been correcting him. She is adamant that she has been correcting her dog for pulling for several years. Something doesn't add up.

When we train a dog, regardless of what we do or what action we take, we really can't call our method a correction unless it fixes the problem. It will be Buster that defines whether we delivered a correction for chasing cats. If his behavior changes for the better, then we corrected him. If his behavior continues then, irrespective of what we did, we didn't correct him. This is not about how hard you yank on a chain. It is about algebra. It is about balancing the equation.

If cat = 100, then our correction must equal 101.

If we can reduce the cat's value to, say, 50 then, we can apply a correction of just 51.

If we can reduce the cat's value to 20, then we can

apply a correction of just 21.

Although I strongly recommend that we use a correction to resolve Buster's chasing habit, that doesn't mean that I want to smack the heck out of Buster. The least amount of intervention that I can put in the system and still change Buster's behavior would be my preference.

Here is a visual representation of the threshold we must overcome to change Buster's behavior if he values cat chasing as worth 100 units.

Motivational Units	
100	Threshold we must reach to truly correct the dog
75	
50	Nagging Zone – we do something,
25	but not enough
0	to change the dog's behavior

For any behavior there is a threshold. If we correct above that level, then the behavior will diminish. If we miss that mark, the behavior will continue. It doesn't matter what we think we did. We will know if we corrected Buster for chasing cats if he stops chasing cats after we deliver what we hope will be a correction.

A Moving Target

The problem is that we don't know where that threshold is. It is constantly moving depending upon circumstances.

Here's an example. I ask you to hold my dog's leash while I go out of the room for a little while. You would probably agree and consider it a fairly easy task. Then I tell you there is going to be food on the floor about 20 feet away, and you must not let my dog eat that food. You may think that won't be too much trouble. Then I inform you that it's not just kibble but, a sizzling T-bone steak. You ponder what size dog this is going to be, and you hope you'll be able to control him. Finally, I say that this dog has not eaten in four days and, he is very hungry. You begin to worry about your capacity to prevent the dog from getting to the meat. With each added bit of information about the situation, you made a mental assessment of what the threshold might be over which you would need to influence my dog to maintain control over him.

There are many things that can contribute to the threshold that we are attempting to conquer. We already know that Buster's cat-chasing threshold is 100, and we have a sense of what that means versus his desire to gain access to his favorite food of all times which is rated as a four. With that information we can determine that Buster has a pretty intense desire to chase cats. Let's say that in comparison my hungry dog might impose 75 or 80 motivational units towards the T-bone on the floor. If I give him a small meal before I bring him to you, his motivation may diminish to around 50 units. If I feed him a complete meal, his desire to get to the steak may go down to 10. Even though he's full, he still is willing to gorge on the real meat. However, if instead of meat I put a dry dog biscuit on the floor, that number may go all the way down to zero. Some dogs have no need to eat dry biscuits if they aren't hungry.

Do you get the point? The threshold that we need to

overcome when correcting a dog is constantly moving. It's our job to assess the dog's impulse and adjust accordingly. If we are using a correction to fix the problem, that intervention must get above the threshold. It would be appealing if we could input less energy into the correction and still have it be effective to change Buster's behavior. How do we reduce the cat's value on Buster's motivational scale?

What's for Supper?

We cannot control certain facets of the equation such as how hungry a dog might be at any given time. A few years ago Robert and I rehabilitated a retriever mixed-breed dog named Maggie. The first day Maggie's owners took her home from the Rescue from which they adopted her, the dog killed the kid's 12 year old cat right in front of them. Although Maggie's new family did not know this, she had come to the Midwest from a Rescue in Arizona. Once they did a bit of research and chatted with folks out west about Maggie's past, it was discovered that she had been running feral for months in the desert. She had taken to killing and eating cats for sustenance. Maggie had a cat killing rap sheet 200 kitties long. That clearly influenced how many motivational units she might score for cat-chasing behavior in particular because to Maggie cats equal survival.

Becoming Proactive

Understandably, there are factors that motivate a dog's behavior that we cannot control, such as a dog's learned habits. However, there are other variables that we can control which have a big impact on whether a correction is effective. Fortunately, we can control two of the most influential elements. The first quality is proactivity. When I was handling Maggie and I knew that there could be a cat around, I paid very close attention to her ears and her head carriage. When I thought that I saw a cat move thirty feet away, I gave Maggie a little warning and then a slight collar check. She may not have even detected the cat yet. However, I wanted Maggie to know that I was in control of the situation and in control of her behavior while I was completely calm and relaxed. I wanted to get her into the right state of mind before she discerned whether that disturbance was a cat or a blowing leaf. Interacting with her that early in the process meant that I was only combatting an interest that scored, say, 25 motivational units. I can match that level of interest with a little pop on her collar or even a touch of my hand to her shoulder or neck area. In human terms it may be like a parent who reaches for a child's hand twenty or more feet before they reach the curb at a street crossing.

Dogs touch each other. If I can emulate the quick jab feeling that one dog might exert upon another and get above that threshold, then I will do that. If Maggie's body relaxed, and she turned her focus away from the direction where we both thought we might have seen something, then I actually corrected her. I fixed her attitude with a poke of my finger or a light snap on her collar. Remember, it's not what we do to the dog but, whether the dog's behavior changes which defines whether we corrected her. To correct means to fix, regardless of the tool or process that we might use.

Being proactive is critical not only to correct a dog but also to convince a dog of your rank. Leaders are highly observant. They address issues in a timely and effective manner. That's why top ranking dogs (and wolves) like to lie on the highest geographical location. In my backyard that place is the back porch. The senior dog lies there so that he can keep tabs on the rest of the dogs. When a kid believes that his mother has eyes in the back of her head, obviously she doesn't have a second pair of eyes back there, but she is incredibly observant because she's the mother. There are no other individuals that are more concerned about the kid than the parents. They see more because they care more. They pay more attention because they have more invested in the safety of the kid. I could develop a process map and produce experimental data that demonstrate the mathematical significance of delivering a consequence sooner than later in the process. This is not an art form. The positive results of acting proactively is measureable. Proactive drivers have less accidents. **It's impossible to be proactive if you are not paying attention**.

Often, the most challenging aspect of teaching someone how to train a dog is to convince them to pay significant attention to effectively win. Winning requires proactivity. When we are dealing with the unique species of dog, training is not just the procedure of using food to positively reinforce behavior or delivering corrections to positively punish the dog. If one enters the relationship with the expectation for obedience to authority, then the idea of delivering a correction above the threshold takes on new meaning. There is a sense of responsibility and accountability that occurs in social species that bolsters the pure mathematics at play.

If you want to take advantage of the effect of your rank over your dog, you need to act like a leader. Leaders take the initiative to set the standard and deliver the consequence for noncompliance. Dogs both trust and respect those individuals who are best able to communicate that they are in charge, in control, and capable of assessing and addressing threats or indiscretions within the family structure. This takes someone who is aware and who is wholly observant and quick to make sound, timely decisions. Being proactive is critical. Being overly stern, loud, or aggressive is counter-productive to the mission. One must learn to be dedicated to the cause without being frantic when taking action. That is often the greatest challenge of all. To achieve vigilance and tranquility at the same time requires practice.

Turn Down the Frantic Meter

The other important attribute that we can regulate when we correct a dog is our level of emotional energy. If you have ever watched a higher ranking dog correct a pup, you will discover that there is no overly arousing passion to the encounter. The message is pure, unadulterated, clear information that is dispensed at close-to-the-perfect level for the offense — just above the threshold to change behavior. Dogs deliver a quick snap then execute a complete purge of any residual negativity.

Dogs don't add extra sentiments like anger, disappointment, disgust, or frustration to their corrections. "I don't hate you, just don't take my rawhide." The message is succinct. Dogs don't lose their cool, well, at least not the truly dominant ones. Dominance is often confused with aggression, but nothing could be farther from the truth. The truly dominant dogs do not need to use aggression to part the waters so to speak. When a dog is dominant, he is about as cool as a cucumber as you can get. He is admired. He does not need to earn respect through acts of violence or intimidation. He already has respect because he is the dominant one. He is dominant because he knows he is dominant. It's that Kung Fu thing happening, again.

I recommend keeping your energy (and the tone and volume of your voice) subdued when correcting a dog. *Turn down the frantic meter.* That is what they expect of higher ranking individuals. You are higher ranking than your dog. Believe, and it will be so.

In order to reduce the number of motivational units that Buster has towards Miss Kitty, we must pay attention and correct proactively without excess emotion, without drama. Then we don't have to input as much energy to get above the threshold to change the dog's behavior. Our goal is to shut down Buster's impulse when he's just considering chasing the cat.

CHAPTER 13

❧∽

REMOTE CONTROL

Even if the title suggests it, this chapter is not about remote shock collars. That technology has an important niche in some aspects of dog training. However, I happen to think that for most of the basics a remote collar isn't necessary. Dogs don't control each other through remote touch. As much as possible, I like to emulate natural canine methods of communication. Since dogs know who just touched them (or who is about to touch them), I prefer to let the dog know it is I who does the touching. That is hard to communicate if the handler is yards away from the dog when it receives the stimulation from a remote shock collar.

Discovering a Dog's Attitude Through Touch

Touching the dog—if even projected down a short leash —reinforces that I have the right to make contact with the dog. A dog's response to my touch can offer some indication about the his attitude. If he chooses to lash back at me, he isn't showing respect for my position. If he were to respond negatively to a remote stimulation I think it would be much harder to use that information to establish the dog's state of mind. He is responding to the physical experience without knowledge of from where it came.

One can learn about the true temperament of a dog by asking him to do what he doesn't want to do and observe how he responds. When using positive reinforcement exclusively, there's no way of knowing how the dog perceives the handler. It's conceivable that he considers the person of lower rank. When one uses a remote collar to provide positive punishment, I feel the same way. There's a lack of understanding about how the dog perceives the information within the context of our relationship. Touching is a right of the upper echelon. Subordinate dogs do not enter the personal space of senior members of the pack. It is simply not socially acceptable.

I often observe dogs controlling each other from remote *without touching*. A higher ranking dog can project that "mom look" from across the yard and shut down a youngster's unwanted behavior. It is that sort of remote control about which I speak in this chapter.

Authentic Remote Control

How does authentic remote control take place? As a general rule dogs warn before they deliver a correction. The senior dog curls his lip, gives a little growl, pins back his ears, or perhaps lowers his head. Those images alone are insignificant. It is when they are followed by a significant event that they gain substance. This is a very rudimentary type of learning that happens in all animals. The relationship between an irrelevant symbol and a significant experience results in an association of the two. The insignificant becomes noteworthy. It allows an animal to use that information to avoid a negative consequence in the future.

Nature is filled with examples of this phenomenon. Stinging insects often don a distinctive striped pattern. Skunks do the same. An encounter with such an animal is memorably paired with the unique display and helps one avoid future awfulness. Toxic fishes are often brightly colored. While rattle snakes need their graphic camouflage to avoid predation, they can still repel an assault through an auditory warning instead. All of these animals rely on the quick learning of potential marauders. Even invertebrates can learn to avoid danger when they perceive a previously inconsequential signal that is paired with an unpleasant experience.

Social species like dogs developed systems to keep peace in the pack without having to constantly make contact with a wayward member of the collective. Controlling a subordinate with a little growl rather than a nip or bite not only prevents the senior member from potentially damaging his own teeth, it also limits the chance that a pack mate will get accidentally damaged. If it requires eight individuals to take down a buffalo, and two are on the disabled list because of an overzealous correction, then everyone suffers. Using symbols rather than direct contact to maintain social order is invaluable to the survival of the species. If a defiant pup can learn that he needs to get a handle on his behavior through the flashing of a few pearly whites, then significantly less energy is expended all around.

Warn First

If we present a warning before we correct a dog for an unacceptable act, the dog quickly learns to change his behavior at the warning signal. I recommend using a simple word or short phrase. The correction must follow if the behavior doesn't change. If the dog heeds the warning, there's no need to follow up with any sort of physical touch. Refraining from doing so is actually quite important to establishing your position.

In the beginning we use a collar and leash to keep the dog present for the lesson and to be certain we can, in fact, deliver a meaningful correction. Soon, however, the leash can be dropped or removed and the dog will remain obedient to the English words. The relationship between warning words and meaningful consequences will have been forged. The word "warning" does not imply one should add any negative emotion or a harsh tone when delivering the signal. Dominant dogs remain entirely calm when they curl their lip, and then they deliver a quick, effective, and emotionless touch or nip to corroborate the meaning of their warning. If you want a pup to "hear" your warnings, you need to stay calm, speak softly, and correct effectively.

A Negative Association?

The PROP suggest that dogs learn to fear people who use a correction-based method because they negatively associate the unpleasant experience with the source of the correction. My experience tells me that dogs learn to not only respect but also quickly learn to trust those who deliver the corrections as long as a consequence is preceded with forewarning. That's how dogs do it. They don't just go around biting other dogs. They give notice first. The very first time they use that method for a specific infraction more than likely the consequence is going to be delivered, but animals learn quite quickly. Few will require a second physical event to alter their behavior.

That is similar to reports from owners of underground electric perimeter fences. Of course, if the dog changes her behavior at the warning stage, then it's important to withhold the correction. At that moment the dog can learn that if she heeds the warning, she can avoid the negative consequence. As the trainer you become a very important entity. You are the one who helps the dog avoid getting a correction because you have knowledge to warn him of the impending doom. A dog that is trained through this process becomes confident, loyal, and trusting in her human leader. She does not learn to fear him.

Cuiado!

Here's a human analogy. Let's say that you are helping your friend with some chores. His father Juan is watching the two of you. Juan doesn't speak any English. Your friend is up on a ladder pulling some boxes down from a shelf. Juan sees that his son seems to be losing his grip, so he shouts, "Cuiado". Immediately thereafter the box falls and lands directly upon your head. Luckily it only contained light weight items. A few moments later Juan notices that there's another box that was dislodged when the first one fell. It begins to fall. Juan shouts again, "Cuiado!" This time you are able to get out of the way and avoid getting hit in the head for a second time. You don't speak Spanish, but you just learned the meaning of "Cuiado." The next time you hear "Cuiado!" you'd know to duck out of the way. Juan's presence in your life has become important to your own survival. You do not become afraid of Juan even though his warning initially was associated with a negative consequence. You learn instead that it's important to listen to him and that he is trying to help you.

Corrections Do Not Have to Be Strongly Aversive

Although it is the accepted term in operant conditioning theory, I chose to avoid using the word punishment when describing consequence based techniques of the Social Compliance method. One reason was mentioned earlier. I think it is a very ambiguous term that is often misconstrued. The other reason is that I believe an individual of a social species is inherently inspired to be, for lack of a better term, social. For that reason a correction does not have to be strongly aversive. This is especially true when the dog that you are trying to influence or teach has a keen sense of obedience to authority. When a puppy is raised properly using Social Compliance techniques, the result is an animal that wants to be right in order to be well received into the collective. He comes to the table with more motivational units to be accepted and fewer motivational units to act out on his individual urges such as cat chasing. His motivation is not so much based on acquiring food rewards but on being worthy of membership in the family.

A correction does not always require physical touch. It just needs to cause the dog to adjust course and fix his wayward behavior. A correction fixes the problem. The stronger the dog's desire to be accepted and partner with a human, the lower will be the threshold above which we need to influence a change in behavior. *The more proactive the trainer is when delivering the correction and the calmer and more definitive he is, the less invasive the correction needs to be.*

The Warning Becomes a Correction

The decision to offer a warning before the consequence, including withholding the consequence if the dog changes course upon hearing the warning, is a very powerful practice. Most dogs quickly learn to adjust their behavior when they hear the warning. In effect the warning becomes a correction. A simple word spoken in a calm and relaxed tone becomes a reliable means of regulating the dog's action. It's so simple and so effective that Robert and I humbly don't understand why everyone doesn't just do it. Nonetheless, many of our clients arrive with sharp tongues or loud and intimidating voices that are shrouded in the sentiments of frustration, disappointment or anger.

I would be remiss if I didn't clearly state that physical contact is commonly required to teach dogs certain lessons. This is often the case with those that have never experienced a human who approaches the relationship in a self-assured, disciplined manner. Dogs touch each other, and they do it with pretty sharp teeth. Their interactions are judicious and effective. When using physical consequences, it's important to make them count so that the next time you need only use your voice to provide the warning.

A warning can be a word or a gesture. It can be a twitch of your shoulder or a slight hand signal. Verbal and visual signals can even be projected across a five acre field and possess the power to influence your dog's behavior. *When the dog believes in your authority, he believes in your authority.* When you inform him that he's about to move into a state of mind (or body) that is outside of the standard you set for the behavior, you are expecting he will acquiesce to a nod of your head even from a substantial distance away.

Most dogs want to know there is someone of conviction that holds higher rank. It certainly makes things easier for the dog. It provides an environment where he can relax and relinquish control to a trustworthy individual who has his own best interest in mind. That is the responsibility of a dog owner in my opinion. It's a job like parenting is a job. You get to reap some extraordinary benefits, but it's not always easy.

Consider, however, that training a dog is significantly more straightforward than raising a child, and he doesn't require a college fund. He is willing to stay home and be your buddy for the rest of his life. Whether his existence is balanced and stress-free is ultimately up to you. Sometimes we have to do what is right not what makes us feel instantly happy. The benefits of having the power to communicate with your dog and alter his behavior through the use of words alone cannot be understated. You don't need to tell the dog what to do but, rather what not to do. That involves substantially less work on your part, as well.

CHAPTER 14

❧❧

SOLVE FOR O WHERE O=OBEDIENCE

You've heard the saying that you have to walk before you run. For that reason it would be silly to take an anti-social, cat-killing dog into a situation in which he could chase down a feline, especially if he had no respect for the person at the end of the lead. The Social Compliance method is something which should be integrated into the human-dog relationship at all levels from the first day the two meet. It is the backbone of the association. One doesn't develop respect by doling out food. You may gain trust and attention by offering treats, but you won't develop a sense of reverence for authority. It is critical to do one's homework in the social department before taking on a feat such as ending potential predatory behavior.

When we were kids, my mother expected us to remain seated at the table, use the utensils properly, put a napkin on our lap, sit up straight, and politely ask for food to be passed rather than reaching over the table. One might wonder why it was so important to practice such manners in the house where nobody was going to see us anyway. However, sometimes we went out for dinner. I'm certain it was far easier to remind us about good manners at home than to teach us proper etiquette in the restaurant. My parents established our acquiescence to their authority on a daily basis by setting high standards for our behavior and reinforcing those expectations at all times, even when it did not seem important. Learning good manners helped prepare us for school and a future job where it would be necessary to accept the idea that a teacher or boss defined the rules which we were expected to follow.

In a perfect world, I would want to establish social compliance with a dog before I attempted to resolve his cat-chasing exploits. If the dog trusts me and is always thinking that I'm in charge, he is less apt to think that he is in charge. He will take cues from me about how he should behave. He will be obedient to my authority. He will have that little bit of worry about whether he is pleasing me that is rooted in his innate need to be part of the family.

A Working Example

Although this book is not intended to be a step by step manual, I feel it is necessary to offer at least one example of how to use the information I have presented.

The basic elements of the Social Compliance method are:

1. Establish a STANDARD for the dog's behavior
2. WARN if the dog begins to break the standard
3. Deliver a CONSEQUENCE for non-compliance
4. Rinse and REPEAT

Most people are able to teach their dog to sit fairly

easily using the positive reinforcement method to lure it into position. It's not the 'sit' through which folks struggle. It is the stay.

The way to get a dog to listen to and obey a verbal command is to emulate the way that dogs teach each other. They don't tell other dogs what *to* do. They tell them what *not to* do. Dogs permit lower ranking pack mates to exist in a state of free-will but expect them to be self-restrained. A pup can mill about, pick up a stick, toss it in the air, drop it, or find a leaf and carry it about in his mouth. He can run, stop, jump, spin, and plop back down again. He can frolic as he pleases until he begins to move towards some boundary that has been set by a higher ranking dog. Often that barrier defines "personal space." An older dog doesn't seem to mind if a pup plays around until it gets a bit too close to running into or over him. Then the adult growls or bares his teeth in warning. If the pup doesn't reverse course but continues to invade the big dog's turf, he will receive a consequence for his actions. If you watch the adult dog throughout that process, he remains unruffled and may even continue working on whatever project was occupying him (scratching, chewing his bone, just hanging out). At the appropriate time, he gives the warning and follows up with the nip if necessary.

Don't Stop Sitting

The PROP seem to think that dog training is about teaching a dog what to do. That could be true if you are trying to train a dog to get into the sit position. However, most people want the dog to stay in the sit position. At that point, in my opinion, we need to switch methods. We need to define "stay" as "don't stop sitting" rather than as an actual exercise called "stay." Understanding this point is very critical. Maybe I should repeat it. We need to define "stay" as "don't stop sitting" rather than the activity of staying.

The activity of staying in position becomes the dog's responsibility. Our obligation is to provide the feedback about boundaries for the behavior as in, "You are about to get up. If you go any further, I will deliver a consequence." This is the same as the underground fence premise.

When utilizing the Social Compliance method, we are usually subtracting the unwanted behaviors from a dog's repertoire of activity. We are not creating behavior. The command to "stay" can be confusing. Are we creating a stay or enforcing a sit? To avoid the confusion, I don't use the word "stay" when training a dog. Once I have given the command to "Sit", nothing further needs to be said. To stay is not an activity that we should teach the dog. To sit is the activity. When we define the lesson in those terms, we no longer feel it is our responsibility to teach the concept of "stay." Instead, we must teach the command to sit and expect that the dog performs that exercise until we release him from that command.

The Standard

Once in position the dog should remain sitting until told otherwise. If you do not adhere to this standard, then the dog will never understand your expectations. You cannot permit the dog to get up and walk away sometimes and not others. Be fair. Set high standards and uphold them. A critical element of the stay exercise should be the expectation for self-control. It's not our job to hold the dog in the sit. It is the dog's job to be self-restrained. We do not need to project our "life-force" at the dog in an attempt to curb his activity.

So often I see folks standing tilted towards the dog with open palms (emulating a stop sign), chanting the word stay over and over again. Their bodies are so stiff that I wonder if it doesn't hurt. They focus on nothing else but the dog. If the doorbell were to ring, they could not leave the dog to open the door. If the phone were to ring, they could not walk away to pick it up. If a pot began to boil over on the stove, they could not race to turn down the heat. These folks act as if it is their energy, their intensity, their power that is holding the dog in place. In a strange sort of way, that's true. If they were to relax, the dog would probably get up and walk away. Why? Because dogs "listen" to body language first. They don't use verbal language to communicate. If you offer a dog body language as an option, it will always pay more attention to that than your words. Dogs don't use verbal language to communicate. Therefore, if you want your dog to listen to your words you must work towards that objective. You should be able to travel about in whatever way you please without triggering the dog's getting up. The handler's normal movements should be part of the training process from the very beginning. The standard is "don't stop sitting." Remember that and you will no longer feel the need to impose your energy on the dog to "stay."

<u>Warning</u>

The reason that I do not typically use the command word "stay" during training is because it is redundant. If I instruct you to sit, I should not have to tell you to stay sitting. What value is a sit without the stay? Sit implies stay. Once I have given the sit command, the assumption is that the dog should remain in that position until told otherwise. That's the standard. The sit command can be considered the warning that it's unacceptable to get up. However, if you want to offer the additional information, you may say "stay" once the dog is sitting. Then, that becomes the warning. *Only say it once.* That is the message that tells the dog of your expectations. A warning should be delivered one time. If the dog does not heed the warning, then the consequence must be delivered. Otherwise, you will create a dog that will simply wait for the second or third or fourth warning word before changing his behavior.

Consequence

In order to deliver a consequence you need to exhibit the qualities of a good dog trainer. Pay attention so that you can correct proactively. Remain calm and relaxed. Watch the dog but not with a stiff posture. Maintain awareness of your dog's state of mind but without undue intensity in your mind or body. Your dog should be relaxed but with the understanding that he is on task. He is working but it's not his job to assess or address any perceived threats, so he does not need to be hyper-vigilant. He may look around and observe. He may not focus on anything in particular with great passion. His body and mind should be untwisted.

If your dog presents any behavior that suggests to you that he is about to break the boundary that you have set (in this case to remain sitting), deliver a consequence that is sufficient to move above the threshold to change his behavior. (See Chapter 12 for further clarification about thresholds for behavior.) Typically, an upward collar correction is used to communicate the boundary for sitting. To learn detailed specifics about how to deliver a collar correction I suggest you read my first book, 4-H Guide: Dog

Training & Dog Tricks (Voyageur Press, 2009).

Rinse & Repeat

Once you have added what you believe was a negative consequence to the equation, it's critical to assess whether it was truly a correction. It's the dog that will tell you whether he received a correction. You don't get to call it that unless you prove that you truly changed your dog's behavior. First, purge any negative sentiments or emotions that you brought into the correction (I call that the rinse). In time you should learn how to deliver a meaningful correction without any negative energy, and the rinse will no longer be necessary. However, it seems to be a natural human tendency to pair some sort of fury, anger, frustration, or disappointment with a correction. With practice and commitment to the idea, you can learn how to deliver a correction and remain relaxed. When you do, the amount of potency you will need to input into your correction will lower significantly.

Set up the same scenario again and challenge the dog to misbehave at the same juncture. Offer your warning word, but do not instantly follow it up with a consequence. If you effectively corrected your dog the first time, he will heed the warning and will change his behavior. He will refrain from crossing the boundary in a self-restrained manner. He should not receive a correction. He will learn that listening to you means that he can avoid a future correction as long as he changes his behavior.

If we apply these simple principles when teaching our dogs tasks like sit, down, and heeling on leash, we will take a dog with the right attitude to the more challenging problems. If our dog believes in obedience to our authority and trusts that we will communicate and effectively enforce standards for his behavior, we can tackle more difficult behavioral issues with greater success.

Back to Buster

Having worked with Buster on basic obedience exercises, such as sit-no-matter-what and walking properly on a loose lead under complete self-restraint, addressing his issue with Miss Kitty will be considerably less nerve wracking. In fact, where Cat once equaled 100 it may now top out at 50 on Buster's motivational scale. That is because through the basic training process he has discovered immense value in maintaining a positive relationship with someone he has learned to trust and respect. He is hard wired to be social, not anti-social. He will shift his loyalty from self-indulgence to behaviors that support his position in the society.

Buster can learn how to sit-no-matter-what in the presence of a cat. Tell him to sit. Enforce the sit. Be proactive in your corrections so that Buster does not move from the sit position. If he is sitting, he cannot be chasing Miss Kitty. Sitting includes staying in that position with the right attitude. Focusing on the cat intensely is not sitting calmly. He should receive a proactive correction for moving from a calm demeanor to a highly focused-on-the-cat state of mind or body. This should be accomplished well before he gets up out of the sit and often at the moment that he turns his head towards the distraction.

Once you work through the problem and effectively teach Buster that your standard for sit-no-matter-what includes when there are felines around, his motivational value to chase cats will decrease even more. Follow the protocol of warn first, deliver a meaningful consequence, and repeat to determine whether you succeeded in truly correcting Buster. Then you will be able to shut down his behavior with verbal communication from a remote location. That is how the process works.

<u>Dominance Is Not a Naughty Word</u>

Most unruly dogs are actually aching to establish a relationship with a calm, composed, confident, competent leader. Except in some of the most extreme cases, one does not need to roll a dog over on his side to establish true dominance. Dominance is not a bad word. It is not about physical power. It is about attitude. Truly dominant dogs rarely fight and seldom even make contact with the lower ranking dogs in their pack. They don't need to do so.

When I see a truly high ranking dog enter an area where other dogs are congregated, it's similar to watching someone like Sean Connery or George Clooney walk into the room. People notice. They sense that someone of distinction has arrived. You can be that person for your dog, but not if your relationship is built on the vending machine principle. You can either be the one that doles out cookies or the one your dog will respect and revere and obey. You can make that choice.

CHAPTER 15

꙳

IN CONCLUSION

It is unfortunate that politics can muddle up something that should be fairly straightforward, like training a dog. I find it simply preposterous that anyone would suggest that a singular method can resolve all canine behavioral issues. At its core it is illogical. Yet that is exactly what the PROP suggest. The idea runs rampant. I see it so often in the press that it's hard to find an alternative option. That's why I wrote this book.

The other day I sent in the registration paperwork for a new puppy. Obviously, my contact information was sold. Within a week I had received junk mail from four or five vendors of pet insurance, veterinary services, and dog trainers. A couple of them were disguised as informational brochures or magazines. Every one of them contained an article that either suggested the only way to train a dog should be through an *exclusively* positive reinforcement process, or they suggested that using corrections in training would ruin the dog.

Clearly, positive reinforcement is a valuable, powerful, essential training method. What I find so odd is the notion that it can resolve any behavioral issue and that using a correction is cruel, dangerous, and in some people's opinion criminal. When I contemplate what it takes to raise a puppy to become a well-mannered, fun loving, polite dog, I find it difficult to believe that anyone really uses a positive reinforcement-only method. I suspect most of the PROP do slip in a correction or two now and again. How refreshing it would be if they would be bold and courageous enough to make that proclamation. Instead, it seems that they spend many resources denouncing the notion of using a balanced approach to dog training. That only leads to confusion and frustration in the general dog owning community including many people who are seeking a solution to their dogs' behavioral issues.

My husband and dog-trainer-extraordinaire, Robert, and I work with clients every day who have been through the wringer with a previous trainer who left them wanting for a solution to common issues. When we give them permission to take control of their dog's behavior, they heave a sigh of relief. Many have said something like, "I would never raise my kids like that, but the dog trainers are adamant about their methods and that we use them." Sadly, some folks come to us in a last ditch effort to save their dog from euthanasia—the "solution" that PROP trainers have informed them is the only option for their anti-social dog.

If the only strategy in one's tool kit is to use food to redirect a dog away from a cat, it's bound to fail. When it fails, the dog becomes increasingly unruly. Maybe a cat gets damaged or the dog causes a traffic accident as he runs across the road on his laser-focused attempt to catch the feline. Perhaps he causes his owner to break her knee cap or tear her rotator cuff as he drags her down the road.

When Cat = 100 and Hotdog = 4, things just don't balance.

Solve for O, where O=Obedience

That is the solution to the equation. Believe that your dog should be socially compliant, and help him to understand your expectations.

I grant you permission to take back the status of Top Dog in your house. In return, your dog will thank you for alleviating all the stress he has been experiencing. If your dog has been presenting anti-social behaviors, he may believe that he is responsible to assess and address all the threats in the world. He may feel that he must claim you as his own and guard you from the evils of your neighbors, their cat, or even your own spouse. When you reclaim the position of Number One, you will afford your dog a more relaxed attitude and a most tranquil existence.

In this book I hope that I have not only shed light on the damaging after-effects of the outrageous rhetoric of the PROP, but that I have offered a logical, sensible, easy to execute, dog-friendly alternative. It is, after all, the closest process to the way that dogs communicate with each other. No other method makes more sense to a dog.

There is science behind the operant conditioning training methods—*all of them*. Remember, we are dealing with a very unique species, one that is so integrated into our own world that it's hard to envision human existence without it. They fit into a niche of human society that can be filled by no other animal. They deserve special consideration because they are special. There is nothing else like the relationship between a human and a dog.

Developing the proper rapport with a canine companion demands more than a training technique. It also requires art, intuition, an understanding of their distinctive status, patience, and love. That love must come from the parenting place in our hearts, that place where we selflessly give what they need—not simply take what we want.

Life is about balance. It is one big algebra equation. Finding poise and equilibrium is the key to developing the best possible connection with your dog. He is not a dolphin. He is the most noble of beasts which developed both alongside us and yet, at the same time, in tandem. Dogs are designed to willingly follow our leadership; therefore we must cultivate leadership skills in order to provide stability and symmetry in our relationship with them. Your dog will thank you when you finally begin to speak his language.

Man and dog is a partnership like no other—forever entwined. They are such a gift to us that it seems only reasonable to reward them with that which they seek most from us: truly benevolent leadership.

ABOUT THE AUTHOR

❧

Tammie Rogers was born in McHenry, IL in 1960. She is the middle of three daughters of John and Carol Johnson. Influential times in her youth included a twelve month residence in South Africa as a foreign exchange student and spending a college semester in Costa Rica.

Tammie graduated from Coe College, Cedar Rapids, IA in 1982 with a degree in Biology. She went on to spend twenty years working as a scientist in academia and corporate America on projects as diverse as basic hearing research to the development of Thyroid Monitoring products.

After residing in Chicago for several years she acquired a small farm in southern Wisconsin where she raised sheep and ducks which she used to train her first Border Collies for herding competitions. She also offered beginner obedience and herding lessons while maintaining her career as a biologist.

In 2002, after having trained and trialed numerous dogs in competitive obedience and herding for nearly twenty years, she turned a hobby and part-time job into a full time profession. She retired from corporate life to launch DarnFar Ranch-a full service, professional dog training facility in Brownstown, IL.

With her husband, Robert, she offers obedience classes and workshops, private instruction, board and train as well as anti-social and aggressive dog rehabilitation.

In 2011 the couple launched Committed Canine, Inc. a not-for-profit organization dedicated to training and education of Service Dogs and their disabled handlers.

OF INTEREST
྾

www.DarnFar.com The Rogers' Full Service Dog Training Facility

www.CommittedCanine.org Non-profit Service Dog Organization co-founded by Robert & Tammie Rogers

www.TammieRogers.com Author's literary website

OTHER BOOKS BY TAMMIE ROGERS
྾

4-H Guide: Dog Training & Dog Tricks, Tammie Rogers (Voyageur Press, 2009) available at most on-line book retailers

T.E.A.C.H. Your Own Service Dog, Tammie Rogers (Lulu.com 2011)

Made in the USA
Lexington, KY
05 March 2014